TOULOUSE
OR NOT
TO LOSE

Diary of an England
Football Fan

TOULOUSE
OR NOT
TO LOSE

Diary of an England Football Fan

Jamie Mash

JANUS PUBLISHING COMPANY
London, England

First published in Great Britain 1999
by Janus Publishing Company Limited,
76 Great Titchfield Street,
London W1P 7AF

www.januspublishing.co.uk

**A CIP catalogue record for this book
is available from the British Library.**

ISBN 1 85756 402 2

Phototypeset in 11.5 on 14 Palatino
by Keyboard Services, Luton, Beds

Cover design Peter Clarke

Printed and bound in Great Britain

Contents

Introduction

The World Cup – the ultimate football competition for players and supporters alike. Ever since it was announced six years ago that the 1998 tournament would be held in France, I decided that I was going. Twenty-five years old, the World Cup just over the Channel, this was the perfect opportunity to do my bit for my country and have the holiday of a lifetime.

The qualifiers were quite a nervous affair, especially because Italy and Poland were in our group. We always get Poland, and have even got them again in the Euro 2000 qualifiers. The thing with the France 98 qualifying groups was that only the top team went through automatically (plus the best of nine runners up), with the remaining runners up going into a two-legged play-off to qualify. England got off to a good start, beating Moldova, Poland and Georgia, but then we cocked up in February and lost 1–0 at home to Italy. I went to that with Dan (my oldest brother), Darren (Darlington fan from Northallerton) and Chris (old mate from college and a Luton fan), and left Wembley feeling well fucked off. We turned it into a good night though, going on the piss around Leicester Square, returning to our hotel at 5 a.m.

After that result Italy were in command of the group, and we were relying on them making a slip up or we'd end up in the dreaded play-offs. As it turned out, we beat Georgia at home and then got a good 2–0 win in Poland (I didn't go so I'll have to next time), which set us up nicely for the autumn. A 4–0 win over Moldova, and Italy only drawing with Georgia, meant that with only one game to go, the crucial decider in Rome, England were on top of the group. Poland and the rest were well out of it, and the fact of it was that if we avoided defeat in Rome, we'd go through and send Italy into the play-offs. We'd have to do it without Alan Shearer though, as he'd injured himself in a pre-season friendly and would be out for months. But we'd beaten Italy 2–0 in the summer's Tournoi de France when Shearer wasn't playing. Ian Wright and Paul Scholes were getting the goals, and the confidence pouring out from Glenn Hoddle and the rest of the England camp was immense.

I didn't go to Italy, mainly because of money but also because I didn't know anyone else who was going. We'd spent the day watching Darlington get hammered 5–0 at Rochdale, and listened to 'Rule Britannia', 'Land of Hope and Glory', 'The Great Escape' and others on the way back, before watching the match in the pub in Northallerton. The beers were flowing and England were basically taking the piss out of Italy. The Italians are even more arrogant than Man U fans when it comes to football, thinking that they've got a divine right to win, especially in Rome where they'd won all of the previous World Cup qualifiers played there over the years.

Then came the sight of Italian police attacking the English fans. Wankers. Anyone who's been abroad before watching England or an English club knows what it's like. Apparently, the Italian fans threw missiles at the English and, when a few English retaliated, the Italian police waded into the English with their batons, helmets and shields, while totally ignoring the Italian fans who were still chucking stuff. That was basically what was happening all over Rome that night, and we expected to hear all the usual 'English thugs on rampage' shit in the press. But no, it seems that a lot of the corporate fans and older spectators including women were caught up in it, and the FA got a report together which they sent to FIFA. The Italians got no more than a slap on the wrist though, but the behaviour of the Italian police was surely a sign of things to come in France.

But it was the best away performance in years by an England team, and after Ian Wright hit the post in the last minute and then Italy nearly scored straight afterwards, England held on for a 0–0 draw that ensured our qualification for France 98. We went mad in the pub celebrating, all deciding instantly that we were going (although only four of us actually did go to France), singing 'We're on the march with Hoddle's army, we're all going to sunny France...' Fucking brilliant! England had made it to the World Cup in France and I would be going.

I'd been abroad plenty of times before, but only once to watch England, which was in Rotterdam in October 1993, for the crucial World Cup qualifier against Holland. Despite the 2–0 defeat which virtually ensured our non-qualification for USA 94, I loved that trip to Holland and it gave me a real taste for watching England away. The atmosphere was mad. Being in a crowd of 5,000 English in a foreign country gives you a feeling of invincibility, even though I did manage to get batted by riot police a couple of times just outside the stadium. All we were doing was singing 'If it wasn't for the English you'd be Krauts!' And of course, I just happened to be right at the front of 200 people, waiting to get into the stadium.

Back to 1998, and the build up to the World Cup seemed to last for ever. Getting time off work was no problem – three weeks annual leave, with the intention of returning after the quarter finals, which, as the draw was made, I was confidently expecting England to be finally getting revenge over Germany for Italia 90 and Euro 96. Fucking Germans and penalties! If there is a God, he's obviously made a rule that England win the wars and Germany win the penalty shoot outs.

Before I carry on, I have to say that there is a lot of strong language in this book, and I have slagged off various groups of people using some politically incorrect stereotypes. But that's just me, I'm politically incorrect, and while I'm not out to offend anyone, I've just used the words that seem appropriate to the occasion. So if you're French, Welsh, Italian, American or whatever, don't take this book personally.

Saving money was more difficult though, given my addiction to drinking beer and following Darlington FC around the country, usually combining the two to good effect. But I managed to save a fair bit in the end and the bank was generous, so the money problem was soon sorted.

But then we hear about the ticket allocations. The French organisers made a real fuck up of that. For the first England game in Marseilles, where the stadium has a capacity of 60,000, they gave the Football Association only 3,500 tickets to distribute initially, although this was later increased to about 7,000. France is in the middle of western Europe. It was obvious that large numbers of fans would travel there for the matches, especially the likes of England, Scotland,

Germany, Holland, etc. But the arrogant French tossers allocated 60 per cent of the tickets to their own fans, who can't exactly be described as passionate when their average First Division attendance is about 14,000. They then allocate 20 per cent to corporate sponsors and rip-off tour operators or official ticket agents, who sell tickets for often ten times their value, leaving only 20 per cent to be divided between the competing nations. What a fucking piss-take! Surely 50 per cent should have gone to the competing nations, 40 per cent to the French, and 10 per cent to the money grabbers and smarmy sponsors who don't really give a fuck about football anyway, other than to make money out of us loyal but often gullible supporters. But in hindsight, the Frogs were quite sly, making 60 per cent available to their own citizens. They knew that this would create a huge black market, and that tickets would be sold to non-French nationals for amounts that far exceeded their face value, and this money would consequently end up in the French economy. Maybe they're not quite as stupid as we thought.

However, even when the CFO (French Organising Committee) realises that they should sell the remaining tickets to non-French citizens, the European Commission steps in and fucks it up (now there's a first!). The CFO wanted to pass on the tickets to the football associations of the competing nations to distribute accordingly. This would most likely have meant me getting tickets for the second and third group games, as well as for the first which I'd already been allocated, seeing as I'd had a priority application form (long standing member of the England Members Club). But no, the EC steps in and says that the tickets must be available to all 'EC citizens', which of course gave us the farce of the tickets hotline. And the CFO made a real cock up of that as well! They had only 90 telephone operators, but 50 of these were to take calls only from within France. Cheeky bastards. The result was something like half a million calls in the first five minutes, and the line was virtually permanently engaged for the two weeks that it was open. But having said all that, the Football Association did agree to the ticket allocations over two years prior to the tournament, so despite all the fuss that they made in early 1998, the FA are clearly not blameless themselves.

Anyway, enough slagging off the French (for now). By early June, I'd got a ticket for England v Tunisia in Marseilles, three weeks' annual leave from work, money, overdraft, credit card, ferry ticket, inter-rail ticket, new rucksack and, of course, my new 6 x 3 St George's flag with Darlington FC sewn across it. I'd also shaved my head again to a number one (3mm), and had a recently acquired scar on my head, which I got in Cardiff last season. Couldn't believe it: Darlo at Cardiff for a meaningless end of season game, nine of us on a minibus, few beers, go to the match, six of us sing (the usual Darlo songs, plus 'En-g-land', 'if it wasn't for the English you'd be skint!', and various references to sheep, in response to their anti-English songs), then I go to the bog for a crap, sat there minding my own business, someone kicks the door, then a metal bin comes over the top and cracks me on the head. Bastards! Fucking blood everywhere, and I had to miss the rest of the match to get seven stitches at hospital. Welsh bastards! Soft as shit, chucking a bin on someone having a dump. They probably got a kicking in Darlington in the previous season, when it kicked off in the town and Cardiff got done over. I now hate Cardiff nearly as much as I hate the scum from Hartlepool (Darlo's local rivals, in case you're wondering). Their

Introduction

anti-English attitudes are just pathetic. Mind you, we're no angels.

But it was now the World Cup, time to forget about life in the Third Division and follow England around France. So, along with Mel from Brompton, another Darlo fan, and Matthew, my cousin from north London and an Arsenal fan, who are both 21, I was ready to head off for France and fly the flag for England, Darlington FC, and Osmotherley, my home in England's green and pleasant land. I was half expecting to be getting involved in some sort of trouble in France, with a group of foreigners having a go at England's reputation, but I wasn't too bothered about that. It would just be like any other time, stand up for myself and others I'm with, but I wouldn't be looking for it. I was just going to France for the football and a laugh, like everyone else. The most likely trouble would be with police. Anyone who's been abroad to watch England or an English club knows what it's like. European police just love to intimidate, wind up and generally have a go at English football fans. As well as my own experience in Rotterdam, there's England in Italy, Man Utd in Porto (Portugal) and Leeds in Eindhoven (Holland) in recent years to illustrate this. But I wasn't too bothered about that either; I wasn't planning to do anything to attract the attention of the police, although you usually don't have to.

The language wouldn't be a problem, because I speak French fairly well, mostly from what I learnt at school and the exchange visits I was involved in. I also speak a bit of German, although most sentences I speak involve some sort of obscenity, learnt from another school exchange, and a tiny bit of Dutch. Clever git aren't I! Mel doesn't really speak much French, and Matt's vocabulary extended

xiii

to *bonjour* and *merci*, so I knew it would be up to me to speak the lingo to the Frogs when they couldn't speak English to us. So that was it. We were on our way. And now the story begins...

Day 1, Saturday 13 June

'Well, this is it,' I said to Mel as we stood on Northallerton station. 'Six years I've waited for this.' And didn't everyone know it! I think everyone at work and in my local pub in Osmotherley were sick of me going on and on about going to France, saying stuff like 'only 237 hours until the train leaves Northallerton', or 'this time next month I'll be in Marseilles'. I was like a little kid counting the days to Christmas.

But now the time had finally arrived, and we were buzzing. I was feeling a bit apprehensive, going abroad for three weeks not knowing what we'd be doing day to day, but I was just glad to be going more than anything. The train came on time and we were finally on our way to France, on the march with Hoddle's Barmy Army. We changed trains at York, where we made sure people knew we were going to France, saying loudly, 'We're going to France, I wonder if anyone else here is,' and then it was down to King's Cross, talking about football and France all the way.

A few Jocks came into our carriage for a smoke, and we got talking to them about the World Cup. I asked them who they supported and two of them were Hearts fans and the other two were Celtic fans. It seems funny how Celtic fans can support Scotland when they only seem to have Irish flags at their matches. Fenian scum! I told them that I used to live near Aberdeen, and they replied, 'Sheepshaggers.' They were more impressed when I said that we were Darlington fans. Funny fuckers the Tartan Army. They wear skirts, show their arses to everyone, wear those stupid ginger wigs with a tartan hat on top, get pissed, speak about as coherently as an alcoholic Geordie with a speech impediment, and yet they never get called hooligans no matter what they do, despite constantly slagging off us English. But these lot were a good laugh (when we could understand them), and we wished each other luck, after I'd reminded them of our 2–0 victory over them in Euro 96 (which I attended – fucking loved it).

We got to King's Cross and met Matthew, thus completing the Darlo/Gooner World Cup party, and after a quick tube journey to Victoria, we were on our way to Dover, still talking about football and France, as well as admiring the scenery of the south London slums. When we got to Dover it was absolutely pissing down, but luckily there was a pub about 30 yards from the station. We went in there for a quick pint and watched a bit of Spain v Nigeria on the TV. Spain scored a cracking goal just after the break, but we later found out they lost 3–2. The locals in the pub were a right bunch of twats. Coming in and saying to each other 'Fackin' 'ell mate, fack, fack, fack.' Thick southern bastards!

After the pub we walked 100 yards down the road to wait for the courtesy bus to the ferry port. Some foreign bird asked us when the bus was, and how much the ferry was, etc. I spoke a bit of French to her, but she said she was Italian, so I spoke some of the few words that I know in that weird language, and the other two were already amazed by my linguistic abilities, even before leaving England.

When we got to the ferry port and through customs, we

got talking to a bloke called Val from Manchester (originally Jamaica) – one of the Reggae Boyz. He was a right laugh, even though he was a Man U fan (yes, a Man U fan who lives in Manchester and goes to every game). The bus then took us past the famous white cliffs of Dover (which prompted a quick rendition of the old song) and down to the ferry. We walked up a gangway, on to the ferry, and where were we? The bar! Sound. I was gagging for a pint. So the four of us got the beers in, and stayed in the bar for the whole of the 75-minute journey. I was already outdrinking the others, but that's no surprise.

Val's intention was to travel to all ten of the World Cup venues, and try to get tickets over there. He showed us his itinerary that he'd typed up – dates, venues, matches and even mileage. He was going to Toulouse at the same time as us, for the South Africa v Denmark game, so we said we'd try and meet in a pub called London Town that was listed in the France 98 guide we both had. He became the first person to qualify for the Jamie Mash card, which is just a card with my name, address, phone numbers and e-mail address on. I told him to e-mail me or phone if he's ever up our way.

We arrived at Calais and got on to another courtesy bus which took us to the station in the town. On the way there I started speaking to some French/Algerian person (in French). He had tickets to sell for the England v Columbia game, but wanted 2,000 francs for them (£200), so I started taking the piss and offering 10 Francs (£1). Yet again the others were impressed with my French.

There was a bar joined on to the station, and we went straight in there because we had a couple of hours to spare before the train. There were quite a few other English in there, which meant all the pint glasses were being used and I had to have two halves. Definite photo opportunity – me drinking out of a half-pint glass. I noticed a poster on the wall which caught my eye, probably advertising some drink they sell. It said 'Le Welsh Simple'. Too fucking right, I thought.

As we were sat there, a familiar voice says, 'All right Jamie!'. It was Yogi, one of my brother Dan's mates from York, who I'd not seen for a couple of years. He told us that 12 of them had got to Calais the day before and spent the night in the cells. Apparently, they ended up in a fight with some locals after a barman glassed one of his mates, the police came and nicked every one of them, but left the French alone. I suppose that's why they were all singing 'If you hate the fucking French clap your hands' when we arrived. So now they were getting pissed and heading for Marseilles using dodgy inter-rail tickets.

Most people left shortly after that to get an overnight train to Marseilles, and Val left to get a train to Lille. We were booked on one of the TGV trains that would have given us four hours' drinking in Paris, and get to Marseilles at 7.30 a.m. But when we got to the platform we find out that there are no more trains that night. Apparently there's another station three miles away for the TGV and Eurostar trains. How the fuck were we supposed to know that? So with no more trains to Paris or anywhere, we were stuck in Calais for the night, and we began the search for a hotel. We must have tried at least a dozen, all saying what was to become a familiar phrase, *c'est complet* (it's full), probably just because we're English (not that I'm paranoid or anything). How can hotels in Calais be full? Who would want to stay there, other than people who get taken to the wrong train station by the courtesy bus? Calais is a shit hole.

We met a right bunch of wankers from Oregon, USA,

4

during our search for accommodation. 'Jeez, you guys speak English, that means we can communicate.' As soon as they realised we were English football fans they promptly fucked off. Tossers! But then we met a couple of Canadian girls who were really helpful, chatty and not bad looking. They were from Montreal and were on their way to England after touring around Europe. One of them became the second person to receive the Jamie Mash card, although as I write this, I've still to hear from her. They said they were booked into a youth hostel so we went up there with them and got a room no problem. Sound. It was a decent room as well.

So, once we'd got ourselves sorted with accommodation for the night, it was time to go out and get pissed. The area that the youth hostel was in was fairly quiet, being mainly residential, but we found a bar just down the road among a row of shops. We had a few beers in there, watching a bit of Holland v Belgium on the TV, and telling the barman that *Angleterre va gagner le coupe du monde* (England will win the World Cup). After that we went round the corner to another bar that was much livelier. We got the beers in and got a table, and talked about how shit Calais was, how nice the beer was, what wankers the Yanks from Oregon were, how decent the youth hostel was, and how many goals England would beat Tunisia by. We got talking to some locals on the table next to us. Nothing very interesting, but they soon left when we said we were over there for the football. After a few more beers we decided to do the usual English abroad thing and start singing (just the three of us). All the usual stuff – 'God Save the Queen', 'No Surrender', etc. Strangely enough, most people left shortly after that. First night in France and we'd already emptied a bar. Not a bad start. Some English bloke then said, 'You're not in England now lads.' That was the whole point you daft twat! He thought he was God just because he'd lived in Calais for three months. That makes him pretty stupid in my mind. We decided to do one though, as our vocal chords had had sufficient exercise, and we were quite pissed by then, and the Englishman from Calais was okay, not really worth any trouble.

So we headed off back to the youth hostel, and just couldn't resist another rendition of 'No Surrender' ('Keep St George in my heart, keep me English, keep St George in my heart I pray, keep St George in my heart keep me English, keep me English till my dying day – no surrender, no surrender, no surrender to the IRA-scum'), followed by 'Vindaloo'. We got back to the rooms and fell asleep listening to my World Cup special tape. I'd put the tape together just before going to France, and on it was songs like 'Vindaloo', 'Three Lions', 'This Time', 'You'll Never Walk Alone', 'Oh Sweet England', 'World in Motion', 'God Save the Queen', 'Land of Hope and Glory', 'Jerusalem', 'Rule Britannia', 'The Great Escape', 'Dambusters', 'Match of the Day', plus many more England classics. Not a bad compilation really, and a great way to end the first day in France after a few beers.

Day 2, Sunday 14 June

I woke up early with my head in bits. The first hangover (of many) in France. I woke the other two up by playing 'God Save the Queen'. Nice start to the day. After a crappy French breakfast consisting of bread, black coffee, orange juice and more bread, the three of us headed off down towards the station, singing '...no one likes us, we don't care, we are England, super England...', still a bit pissed from the night before. We got to the station and found that we'd missed a train to Lille by five minutes, so we had to wait another hour for the next one. I needed a dump, so I went to the bog, having to put two francs into a slot on the door, only to find that there's no bog roll and no seat. So I had to go to the station shop and buy a packet of tissues for 10 francs before I could do the business. Even the hand dryer didn't work. Useless French bastards!

We then went down to the platform and got the train to Lille Flandres, with a few other English and some Jamaicans, who were playing in Lens later that day. Some lads there told us that there'd already been trouble in Marseilles with the local Arab youths, with some English lad getting hit by a car and various other incidents, which made us a bit apprehensive. We arrived at Lille after a fairly uneventful train journey. It was absolutely pissing down (again), and we had to walk 400 yards (with a rendition of 'Singing in the Rain') to the Lille Europe station, where we booked onto the 12:17 TGV train to Marseilles. All TGV trains require reservations, so we had to pay a 160-franc supplement to go in first class, as the rest of the train was full.

As we were sat waiting for the train, munching sandwiches and drinking beer, I made the observation that 'there's not been many coppers around since we got to France'. About five seconds later, four coppers walk past with batons and helmets attached, accompanied by four armed soldiers. What a piss take! Anyway, we finally got on the train and relaxed in our first class accommodation. The seats were great – they had a button on the arm which made them slide up and down, which kept us amused for 20 minutes. The TGV trains are very quiet, smooth and fast, which is just as well because their other trains are shite.

Once we were on the move I dozed off for a bit, but was woken up by someone playing 'Barbie Girl', that irritating song that had been released a few months earlier. Tosser! Half a dozen other English were a few seats in front of us and had a CD walkman with speakers. The others with him told him to put 'Vindaloo' on again, so once he did I was wide awake and in the mood for more booze. Mel went off to the buffet car and came back with three bottles of vin rouge (red wine), because they'd sold out of beer. The wine went down well, and once 'Vindaloo' and 'Three Lions' were playing for the fifth time, the others down the carriage asked us to join them, so we did. And of course, it was a perfect opportunity to play my World Cup special tape, which ended up being played for most of the remaining four hours to Marseilles. Someone came back from the buffet and said they'd sold out of booze. You could tell that there was plenty of English on board – one and a half hours and we'd drunk the train dry. So Jon from Sheffield gets out this huge bottle of duty free vodka and the booze problem was sorted for a while.

The booze was flowing, the tunes were playing, we were all singing, and the French countryside drifted past us. A few Millwall lads came and joined us for a bit, and we were having a great laugh. Singing along to 'This Time' ('We're on our way, we are Ron's 22, hear the roar, of the red white and blue, this time, more than any other time, this time...'), 'Vindaloo' and all the rest on that train to Marseilles remains one of the best memories of the World Cup. Fucking loved it! I don't know about the French who'd paid the extra money for first class tickets, only to have us doing their heads in. But we didn't really give a toss about them. The booze soon ran out though, vodka and all, a few people got off at Avignon, including the tosser who kept putting 'Barbie Girl' on, and we started to sober up as we approached Marseilles. And it suddenly looked as hot as fuck outside.

We finally arrived at Marseilles just before 6 p.m., not knowing where we'd be staying. The station was a bit chaotic with loads of other English without tickets or accommodation. Mel bought a ticket from someone for 1,000 francs, just in case he never met the agent he'd bought his from, but ended up selling it on for the same price later. The plan was to go to the campsite at Cassis, because we thought all the hotels were full. But we were told that Cassis was miles away, and the campsite on the beach sounded a bit dodgy for leaving our bags there, especially with the number of Arabs in the area and the trouble that had gone on during the night before. We'd also heard about how dodgy the Arab quarter of Marseilles was, so we decided to try for a hotel. The tourist information office at the station phoned around the hotels in the area. They gave us the address of one about six miles away where there were a few rooms left, so after a £20 taxi we got to the hotel and got a room for the three of us, one on the bed and two on the floor. Me being an unlucky fucker when it comes to tossing coins, I ended up with both nights on the floor. But at least we'd got somewhere to stay for the duration of our visit to Marseilles.

It was then time to get another £20 taxi back into town, to try and meet up with Sven and Jon from Northallerton, who we were supposed to meet up with two hours earlier at O'Mally's Irish pub in the Vieux Port. The taxi dropped us off just down the road from the Vieux Port because of the traffic, so we ended up walking past a few hundred Tunisians listening to some crappy Arab music. We headed for an even bigger crowd singing 'Rule Britannia' and 'No Surrender'. 'Looks like we've found the Irish pub,' I said. There was a good crowd outside, mostly quite hard looking, so any feelings of paranoia soon went. Not that I was worried walking through a bunch of Arabs, we could have handled ourselves, until the police would have waded in and nicked us for being English. Mind you, I don't think that walk would have been possible two hours later.

We found Sven and Jon inside O'Mally's and got some beers (in plastic glasses) which we took outside – too packed and hot inside, plus all the singing was outside. The Irish flag hanging outside the pub was soon pulled down. For some reason it wouldn't burn, so it was thrown into the harbour, accompanied by a rousing rendition of 'No Surrender', all good-humoured stuff. Everyone was just getting pissed and having a laugh.

After a few more beers we noticed something going off

down the road. A few Tunisians tried to have a go, chucking bottles and stuff, and about 50 lads chased them back down the street. There wasn't really much point in bothering to go down there, 'cos I would've only got nicked or pictured on the front page of *The Sun* or something. Then the riot police moved in firing tear gas canisters. We couldn't really see all that well what was going on down the far end, but this went on for about 20 minutes, England charging, police firing tear gas, Tunisians throwing bottles which the police ignored, English charging, more tear gas. The funny thing was that the wind blew the tear gas away from us lot and back down to the police, local Arabs and various families eating meals. Most people just ignored it after a while, although I was a bit wary of the Arabs coming round the other side of the pub, via the back streets, seeing as they were mostly locals. We wanted to stay there, seeing as we had some live entertainment, but Mel had to meet a ticket agent at a hotel near the beach, so the five of us headed off to find a taxi.

Talking to some other lads the next night who'd stayed down there, apparently the police closed the Irish pub later on and moved everyone out of the area, despite a growing number of local Arabs hanging around. They said that the Arabs were down every street in the area, not just Tunisians but Algerians and Moroccans as well, trying to have a go. Whenever the English mobbed up and charged them they'd run away, but there was always another mob of Arabs waiting, covering the alleys and backstreets. Four English got stabbed, two in hospital, one with his throat cut. Apparently the cut was that fine and he was that much into the fighting that he didn't even know he'd been cut at first, he just collapsed in a pool of blood. As far as I know he's okay

11

now. The English that were involved in that trouble were just retaliating, defending themselves from wankers having a go at our reputation, although a few of them were obviously there purely for the fighting.

But that is no excuse for our shitty, fucked up, retarded media to call us all (the 40,000 English in Marseilles) a disgrace, scum, thugs, hooligans, and whatever else. Those shitty journalists photograph someone who's been hit over the head with a bottle or truncheon and label him a thug. It's scum papers like *The Sun* and the *Mirror* that are a disgrace to the country not us. It's the Arab scum of Marseilles that caused the trouble, not us. If we didn't have to leave the pub to meet the ticket agent, we would have been involved in the trouble later on, with no choice but to fight to defend ourselves against the dirty Arab knife merchants. Does that make me a mindless thug? Of course not. Even Tony Blair apologises to the French government and other politicians slag us off. What the fuck do they know? I've never been an admirer of Tony Blair, but I'd never have thought he was a *Sun* reader. Surely the French authorities should have apologised to us, for the behaviour of their police and north African immigrants. I'm sick of the media churning out the same old shit about us English football fans. So fuck off you tabloid scum!

Anyway, I'll take a break from slagging off the media and get back to what the five of us did after we left the Vieux Port. We got a taxi to the hotel, got the beers in and Mel waited around for the ticket agent. On the way up there, the taxi driver said that he hates the local Arab population, and they always cause trouble in the city. He added that they'd started the trouble and the English were not to blame. Yogi (who we'd met in Calais) said later that a French copper said, 'It's good that you English come here and fight with the Arabs, we hate them and they always cause trouble. We'd like to arrest them all but there would be riots for three days after you go.' Are you listening Tony Blair? Find out the truth before you go and embarrass our nation by apologising for something that wasn't our fault.

While Mel was sorting the ticket out we watched a bit of football on the TV and then Arsene Wenger turns up, the Arsenal manager. Matt was dead chuffed, being an Arsenal fan, and we got some photos taken with him. He was a bit of a miserable sod though. Once Mel was sorted with his match ticket, we decided to try and find this English pub called the Red Lion that everyone was on about. The ticket agent said it was just along the sea front, so we decided to walk it. Sven and Jon got a taxi back to their campsite, so me, Mel and Matt headed off in search of the Red Lion. We came to the big screen where they were showing the Jamaica v Croatia match, so we stopped there for a beer and a hot dog. After that we walked for ages but still couldn't find the Red Lion, so we stopped in a pub down the road with loads of tables outside and had a few more beers. I was getting quite pissed by that time, and I spent most of the time sat outside drooling over the waitress who worked there. Short skirt, lovely legs. I seem to have a thing about barmaids or waitresses. Must be something to do with them giving me beer. There was a small mob of English walking past making noise, followed by some local Tunisians about ten minutes later, but nothing was happening really.

After that we decided to head down the road for a taxi back to our hotel, but couldn't see any around. We saw four Tunisians and I said, '*Angleterre va gagner demain*' (England will win tomorrow), and then got talking to some Barnsley fans. We walked along with them and then got to a camper van that was parked up, surrounded by loads of Brummies who were blasting out some tunes – the usual stuff – 'Vindaloo', 'This Time', and that old favourite from *The Italian Job*, 'The Self Preservation Society'. We decided to join them for a dance about and a singsong, and the Barnsley lads went off to their car across the road to get a crate of beer. Sorted! So we spent the next two hours drinking, singing, dancing and flying the flag of St George, having a right laugh. Nearly every car that went past sounded it's horn at us, which was met with a load of abuse. Some kids walking past even got mouthy, but they were soon chased off. French/Tunisian fuckers! I think the highlight was standing on the wall (and falling off several times) and singing 'Let's go fucking mental', and then jumping all over the pavement, dancing around with the 20-odd other pissed-up lads (and a few lasses) from the West Midlands, Barnsley and Plymouth (one Argyle fan on his own – we forgave him for beating us at Wembley in 96). Such fun!

We eventually went off to get a taxi, and got back to the hotel after the stupid taxi driver got a bit lost. Soon fell asleep after a day of beer, wine, vodka and more beer. I was fucked!

Day 3, Monday 15 June

I woke up feeling like shit, my head was in bits. To make things worse, the light in the shower didn't work, so I was in almost total darkness. Still, I was buzzing 'cos it was the day of England's first match of the World Cup, and we soon got a taxi down to the stadium with three others who were staying at the hotel.

We went to a bar just down the road from the stadium, where there was loads of other English. I could only manage a glass of water though, with the state I was in. I even had trouble asking for that. Trying to speak French when you're absolutely fucked from the night before isn't easy. Especially when you want a glass of *eau*. What a stupid name for water! It's more of a grunt than a word for the most important liquid to life on earth. Anyway, I managed to get some water, and went outside to savour the atmosphere. A mob of Tunisians then walked past, making loads of noise, and I thought it might kick off after the previous night's events. But it was all just good-humoured stuff. It's funny really, us English tend to be quiet during the daytime, and get loud in the evening. Must be something to do with booze. Half a dozen buses of England fans then drove past us, probably from the airport, with an over the top police escort. There was singing coming out of every bus, each one being met by a loud cheer from us lot outside the cafés.

After a while we decided to walk down the road to have a look at the stadium. The match was due to kick off at 2.30 p.m., with the gates opening at 12 a.m., and it was now about 11.30. There was a good atmosphere, everyone excited by the occasion, and the sun was shining brightly. The three of us had tickets from different sources (Football Association and ticket agent), so we all ended up in different parts of the ground. Mel was in the main stand, below all of the press boxes and quite near the front, Matt was at the top of the stand opposite, in one of the official FA sections, and I was behind the goal to the right of the main stand, right at the top, with the main section of official FA ticket holders. We walked around for a bit and took some photos of ourselves with my Darlo flag, and decided to go in shortly after mid-day, after arranging where to meet up later.

The weirdest thing was that when I got searched at the gates, the copper took the lid off my plastic bottle of water and chucked it away. What the fuck for? As if a little plastic bottle cap could be used as a weapon. They did this with all drinks bought inside the stadium, probably so you drink up quicker and go and buy another bottle of water for 15 francs (£1.50). Bastards! Anyway, I walked past a stall selling World Cup souvenirs, mostly hats and things. I wanted a sunhat but they only had baseball caps for £15 so I didn't bother. What a fuck up that turned out to be. I'd shaved my head to a number one (3mm) three days earlier, so the top of my head was completely exposed. No hat, no hair (hardly), no shade, no suncream (I forgot about my face and the top of my head). So I ended up getting burnt to fuck in the Marseilles sun, the symptoms of which I'll describe later. 'But the phrase 'mad dogs and Englishmen go out in the midday sun' springs to mind.

16

Anyway, I got to the stand that I was to be in, and ended up walking a few hundred steps to within a few seats from the top of the stand. I was knackered. First thing was first, put my flag up. I found a good place on the fence at the back, next to two similar flags, one Notts County and the other Reading. I stood talking to some Reading fans for a bit, and then noticed Mel's flag down at the front of the main stand.

Still feeling rough from the night before, I headed for the bog for another shit. I had to walk all the way down to the bottom of the stand, outside and back in, before finding the bog. To make things worse, as I walked out of the stand, I saw an overweight middle-aged scruff wearing a scum shirt (that's the monkey-hanging scum of Hartlepool). I was disgusted. Oh well, I thought, I'll sit down and have a good dump now. But I was in for a shock. I went into the bogs, opened the door, and what did I find? A toilet? No! A fucking hole in the floor with a roll of bog paper on the wall. I was supposed to shit in that? It was more like a fucking shower cubicle. The stupid, fucked up, retarded French bastards. Where is the logic in it? Surely they can see the advantages of the good old toilet, with a seat on it? But I was desperate, so I had to lean back and squat over this hole, whilst squeezing out another watery shit. Fucking lovely! So it was then back to the top of the stand, which left me knackered again.

Although the size of the Stade Velodrome is quite big, with a capacity of 60,000, I thought it was a bit crap really. Marseilles is a fucking hot place, especially in June, so there should be a roof on each of the stands to keep everyone in the shade. The seats are just crap bits of plastic with no backs on or anything. And there's no refreshments or toilets other than right at the bottom of the stand, which is a bit of a cunt when you're right at the top, and feeling as rough as I was.

But apart from that, the stadium's quite impressive, and it was a good feeling to be at a World Cup venue, awaiting England's first match of the tournament. As the stadium began to fill up, it became apparent that there was more English there than the official FA allocation of 7,000. More like 40,000. Obviously loads of tickets had been bought through various agents, official and unofficial, and from ticket touts in Marseilles. Someone in front of me had a huge cardboard photo of Des Lynam on a pole, with a St George's flag draped around it. Sound as fuck! Apparently, back home on the BBC, when introducing the coverage of the match, Des started by saying 'Good afternoon. Shouldn't you be at work?' Good bloke is Des. Anyway, the Tunisians were mostly down the other end, with a few in the main stand, but there was probably no more than 5–6,000 of them, which is surprising given the large local Arab population, and the amount there seemed to be outside. They were making loads of noise before the match, but it was obvious that they'd be fucked by the time the match started. The PA bloke said that in the spirit of the World Cup, he'd play some music from the competing nations. The Tunisians got some of their crappy Arab shite, and we got 'Candle in the Wind'. He should have played 'Vindaloo' or 'Three Lions'. Still, he did play 'Carnival de Paris', which got us all singing.

So, it was soon 2.20 p.m., the stadium was full, St George's flags and Union Jacks on virtually every fence or wall of each stand, and the teams came out. This was it. England in the World Cup! Come on! The teams were lined up, and the band started playing 'God Save the Queen', accompanied by 40,000 screaming Englishmen ('God save our gracious

Queen, long live our noble Queen, God save the Queen – no surrender – send her victorious, happy and glorious, long to reign over us, God save the Queen'). And then the match was underway. We had a few decent runs early on, especially by Paul Scholes, but not that many chances to start with. Teddy Sheringham hit a blistering volley against the bar, but he had a fairly quiet game apart from that. As half-time approached England had several good chances, especially an effort from Scholes and we also had a penalty appeal turned down.

We then had a free kick just outside the area, a few yards from the goal line. The ball was crossed in, up pops Shearer at the far post and the ball's in the net. Yeeeeeaaaas! We went mental! I fell over, got up again, carried on going mental, before joining in shouts of 'Shearer, Shearer, Shearer'. I started a rendition of 'You're not singing any more', before joining in 'One–Nil to the England. And then it was half-time. I went all the way down to the bottom of the stand again, to get another over-priced bottle of much needed water, and to escape from the scorching sun. I was feeling rough even when the match started, but going mad celebrating Shearer's goal made me feel much better. Cheers Alan!

After that it was back up to my seat (knackered again after all those steps) ready for the second half. There was a good atmosphere in the stadium, despite there being no roof on three of the stands, and everyone feeling the effects of the heat. The England Supporters Band were down near the front of the stand, and they kept on playing 'The Great Escape', which everyone joined in with. It was sound! 'Der der, der der der-der der...' And then there was all the usual favourites, 'En-g-land', 'Football's Coming Home', 'English, and We're Proud of it', and 'Vindaloo'. I definitely think that England had the best supporters of the World Cup, in terms of taking over the stadiums and singing our hearts out, with the best songs and most flags. At one point of the match, a load of French in one of the neutral sections kept starting a Mexican Wave. Most people joined in with it around the stadium, including a lot of other English, but when it came around to our section which was exclusively for the England Members Club, we all just sat there, raised our right hand and did the wanker sign, accompanied by a load 'aaaahhhhhhrrrrrhhhh'. This went on for about five minutes, and reminded me of exactly the same thing happening in Rotterdam five years earlier – Mexican Wave all the way round the stadium, gets to the 5,000 English who respond with the wanker sign, and the Dutch booed us.

Back on the pitch, England carried on where they left off in the first half, creating a few decent chances. One of the highlights was David Batty trying to do an overhead kick to clear the ball, but instead kicked a Tunisian player in the head. Funny as fuck! Tunisia played a bit better later on, although they didn't seriously threaten our goal, before Michael Owen came on for Sheringham and got a great reception from the fans. Right at the end of the match, Scholes got the ball on the edge of their area, got a view of the goal, and launched an unstoppable shot that curled beautifully into the top corner. Time to go mental again, except I avoided falling over this time. So it finished 2–0, although it could have been more, and everyone was happy after a comfortable victory.

I left the stadium and got to where I was to meet the other two. Mel was already there, and Matt turned up about 15 minutes later, after being made to take a long detour from the other side of the stadium. We got to the area of the bar we went to earlier, and tried to decide what to do, feeling rather indecisive. There was a couple of lines of French riot police stood at the side of the pavement, looking ready for action. Mel couldn't resist a quick photo of them, and then I decided that I wanted to be in the picture. I went over to the coppers, said *'bonjour'* but they just stared at me, so me and Matt stood right in front of them while Mel took our picture. What miserable twats they were. After that some tosser of a French journalist started talking to us. No mention of 'did you enjoy the match' or 'are you enjoying your time in France', he just wanted to know if we'd seen the trouble in the Vieux Port the night before. We told him that we had, that the Tunisians started it, and that most people ignored it and are in France for football, drink and a laugh.

After sitting around for a bit among loads of other English, we decided to head down the road to look for a bar. We all made a quick phone call home, just to say that we'd not been nicked or stabbed or anything, knowing how much over the top the news would be back home after the weekend's events in the city centre. We finally found a bar that was open, and it was full of English, singing and drinking, with a few people sat outside as well. Sound!

The bar owner searched us for weapons on the way in, which was a bit weird. As we were waiting at the bar, the waiter walked past carrying a tray full of empty glasses and bottles. He knocked into someone, and the glasses went crashing onto the floor, one after the other. Funny as fuck! Everyone laughed their heads off, before someone started up an alternative version of 'Vindaloo', which ended 'you're gonna drop one more than us ... you're sacked'. Shortly afterwards this cockney at the bar managed to drop his glass while laughing at the waiter. I looked at the owner and his hand was shaking like fuck. He was shitting himself. Poor French bastard. He had about 30 English inside his pub, laughing at his clown of a waiter who was clearing up the glass, and about another 20 outside. All this after hearing endless stories about *les hooligans anglais*.

I finally got a beer and we sat outside at one of the tables. The other two didn't bother with a beer because it was 20 francs for a bottle that was less than half a pint. I was desperate though, in need of more beer to sort me out. As we were sat there, there was the constant noise of police sirens doing our heads in. It was even worse than on Charing Cross Road after the England v Scotland game in Euro 96. We couldn't make our minds up about what to do next. The other two wanted to go to the beach area where the big screen was, but I wanted to drink nearer to our hotel, as I was still feeling a bit rough. After another beer we decided to head down towards the Vieux Port, where we were the night before, and set off on a long walk. As we left the pub, a big Dunstable flag went up over one of the windows. I think most people in the pub were West Ham, Leeds and Luton. Nice mix!

There were a few other English walking ahead of us, but as we got nearer to the centre after about half an hour's walk, an English couple going the other way said, 'Don't go to the Vieux Port, the riot police have closed it all off.' Sounds fun, I thought. We kept on walking down the road, but then noticed that there were no other English in sight, not even any French, just dirty looking Arabs. Bollocks! We'd walked straight into the Arab quarter, and could almost feel everyone staring at us. Time for a taxi and get out of that shit hole. The taxi driver was watching football on a small TV with an ariel sticking out of the window, which I managed to trap in the door and damage. Ha ha! We soon got back to the hotel, where we crashed out for a bit in the room and watched football on the TV – the England match replayed on Eurosport and then a bit of Romania versus Colombia. It'd been boiling hot that day and we needed to cool off for a bit.

At about 9 p.m. we decided to go out for some beer and food, and found a bar/restaurant just down the road from the hotel. We had a quick beer and then went next door for something to eat. I ordered a pizza, but when it came it was more like a poppadam thickness nan bread with a bit of cheese on top. And it took about 10 minutes longer to arrive than Matt's spaghetti Bolognese, which smelt gorgeous. I had some of his spag bol on my pizza, to give it more substance. Still, I was hungry and soon stuffed it down, before a couple of Villa fans came and joined us for a bit, finishing off Mel's wafer-thin pizza which he didn't like at all. I paid for the meal on my Visa card, which took ages because the staff couldn't work out how to use the credit card machine, until one of then told the others to type in the amount and then swipe the card. Thick twats! They were okay though. All the staff in there were a good laugh, as we were to find out later.

There turned out to be about a dozen other English in there, and we got talking to some Southampton and Chelsea fans. They'd been down in the Vieux Port when it kicked off after we'd left during the previous night. The news came on the telly, showing pictures of the trouble in the city centre, which got everyone's attention. They then showed highlights of the England match, which produced loud cheers in the bar when the goals were shown, as well as

David Batty kicking the Tunisian in the head. One of the locals was then desperate to play one of us at table football, so Matt obliged and thrashed him, as did one of the others.

The beer was going down well and, as I returned to the bar for another, I asked the staff if they had a larger glass (speaking French of course – it turned out that none of the French in there spoke English). They found what must have been the only pint glass in the bar, and I was happy. I'd got my pint glass, and I'd make sure that I'd be the only one using it that night.

There was quite a good mix of us in there – Darlington, Arsenal, Chelsea, Southampton, Liverpool, Carlisle, Villa, Wolves, and whatever else, all getting on well. By midnight the singing had started. All the usual stuff, such as 'Rule Britannia', 'God Save the Queen', 'En-g-land', 'Vindaloo', 'The Great Escape', 'Dambusters', 'Stand up if You Hate Germans'. The locals seemed a bit apprehensive at first and it looked like they'd asked a few people to stay back in case we kicked off. But we were just there for a laugh as they soon realised, and although the staff or locals couldn't speak any English, we got on really well with them, mainly through me speaking French. I asked them to sing the French national anthem, and they duly obliged, singing with pride, accompanied by us lot going 'la-la la la' etc. Then it was our turn, and we all sang 'God Save the Queen', with one of the locals conducting us.

Whenever it went quiet for a bit, all it would take is for someone (usually me or the scouser) to look at one of the others, bang their glass on the table, and go 'na-na na…', which led to everyone bursting out into another chorus of 'Vindaloo'. One of the lads had a 'Vindaloo' song sheet, and showed it to the local with the dodgy Saddam Hussein style tash who got beat at table football, and tried to get him to sing along with us. He couldn't quite manage it though. Someone else showed him a picture of Jurgen Klinsmann and some other German footballers, and we explained what we meant by 'Stand up if You Hate Germans' (not that I do, given the fact that I've got friends in Germany from the old school exchange I used to be involved in). The local then promptly returned to the bar, thought about what we'd said, and then began jumping up and down on the spot, thumbs pointing downwards, chanting 'Germany, Germany, *enculez* (fuck off)!' Nutter! I think the highlight was when the 15 or so English and half a dozen locals were walking around, arms stretched out to the sides, singing the tune from 'Dambusters'. Fucking brilliant!

I learnt a new bit of French when I was there – *je suis seul*, which means 'I am drunk'. It came in useful. The staff decided to close the bar at about 3 a.m., so we shook hands, thanked them for a good night, and headed back to the hotels. But we weren't finished yet.

All of us were staying in two hotels which were virtually opposite each other. I went back to our room to get the tunes, someone else got some vodka, someone else got some beer, and someone else got some port. We all met up by a wall between the hotels and then got pissed and listened to the tunes. I particularly enjoyed the vodka. One of the lads soon went back to his hotel to crash out, feeling a bit fucked. Five minutes later a huge Wolves flag comes out of a window, accompanied by a shout of 'Will you lot fucking shut up, I'm trying to sleep here' (in a broad Midlands accent), and then he promptly disappeared back inside with his flag. That was Hollis, who we'd later see in Toulouse.

By 5 a.m. we were all feeling fucked and it was getting

light. All of a sudden a police van arrives and three coppers get out. We were going anyway, so I said, '*Nous allons maintenant*' (we're going now), and '*Nous restons la bas et la bas*' (we're staying over there and over there), pointing at the two hotels. They were okay with us and I even shook hands with one of the coppers, before going back to the hotel to crash out. Before leaving, we'd said to the others to try and meet at the London Town pub in Toulouse over the weekend.

What a fucking great night that was, especially in the bar. It's typical though that no journalist wants to hear about such high points in Anglo-French relations, just stories of *les hooligans anglais*. But for me and everyone else there, that night remains one of the highlights of the holiday. I was really enjoying this World Cup lark.

Day 4, Tuesday 16 June

Another day, another hangover! We still felt good though, after England's win and our piss up down the road. But then after a quick shower, I noticed funny lumps on my head. I rubbed my hand through my hair (what there was of it). Urrrhh! Something wet and sticky. And crumbly. Dead skin. Aaaarrrrgghh! Sun blisters. The top of my head was as scabby as fuck! Little blisters oozing with puss and crumbly dead skin. Fuck! I thought I could feel the top of my head burning, as well as my face which had turned a bit red. I knew I should have worn a hat. Oh well, 'mad dogs and Englishmen go out in the midday sun' (with a skinhead, no hat and no suncream)…

Anyway, after the horror of all that, we went downstairs with our rucksacks to get a taxi to Marseilles station. We'd arranged to meet Sven and Jon at the station, and the plan was to travel to a town called Fréjus, about 80 miles east of Marseilles, where a girl called Helen worked on a campsite. She used to work at the same place as me, Sven and Jon, although I didn't know her all that well. I think Jon knew her the best.

Anyway, we got down to the train station and spotted a Sunderland shirt. That was Sven. We got over there and he said that they didn't recognise me at first – I'd borrowed Mel's spare sunhat and was wearing sunglasses. But then they spotted my t-shirt – 'Darlo on Tour – World Cup 98', with a St George's flag on it. They told us that they'd watched the England match on the big screen down at the beach, where we'd seen on the news that it had kicked off a bit. They told us a familiar story – England score, England fans celebrate, dirty fucking Tunisian scum throw bottles and seats from the temporary stand, England get stuck into them, riot police have a go at the English, using tear gas as usual, while ignoring the Tunisians who started the thing in the first place. Who gets blamed? The English of course! If there's a drought in India, or a tornado in the USA, we'd still get blamed for it. If there's a problem in the world, just blame the English, especially those nasty soccer hooligans. What a load of bollocks! Fucking press. Fucking French. Fucking Arabs. But we won 2–0, so ha ha you twats! Sven and Jon said they'd got away as soon as the pigs steamed in, and watched the second half in a hotel bar. I showed them my fucked-up head, told them about our night in the bar, and then we went to our train.

The journey lasted about an hour and a half, and there were some quite scenic views along the way, especially the Mediterranean Sea contrasting with the hills and clear blue sky. Another hot day in the south of France, although I was still a bit too tired from the night before to take much in. It was good though, the madness of Marseilles behind us, sat chilling out on the train, with another two and a half weeks of travelling, football and beer ahead of us.

The train got to St Raphael and we got a ten-minute bus ride to Fréjus. I'd spotted a decent-looking bar just before the bus stop, so we walked back down the road for a drink. There were loads of tables outside, in the shade of a couple of trees, with a view of a roundabout on one side and a ruined castle on the other. Nice place to chill out for a bit.

As the beer started flowing we started talking about Sunderland's play-off defeat a few weeks earlier, when they got beat on penalties at Wembley. What a fucker that must have been for Sunderland fans (like Sven and Jon), missing out on the Premiership by one penalty kick, after finishing well clear of the team that beat them, Charlton. Darlo's play-off final defeat two years earlier was bad enough, but at least we never had the agony of losing on penalties. That just happens with England.

It was then time for a dump, another beer, and a cheese sandwich, in that order. After the previous day's experience in Marseilles, I got a bit of a shock when I went into the bog. Not only was there actually a toilet there, it had a seat on it, and on the seat was a plastic cover that moved round to a fresh bit with the press of a button. Fucking French! You shit in a hole in one town, and sit on a fresh plastic-covered seat in another. I wish they'd make their minds up.

Anyway, enough talk about shitting (for now). Had a great sandwich after that, washed down with a beer, and then we headed off towards the town centre. It was fairly hot, so we settled down at a bar near the centre, in a small square with a fountain in it.

We sat outside in the shade, wearing sunhats, looking sunburnt, and ordered four large and one small beers. Spot the English! We were there for quite some time, enjoying the late afternoon sunshine, getting slowly pissed and watching the world go past. I ended up reading the Marseilles paper from the day before, which had loads of photos of Sunday night's events. Although it was naturally in French, I understood most of it. Same old crap, *les hooligans anglais,* but at least they said that the local Arabs were the cause of a lot of the trouble, and didn't call us scum, animals, a disgrace and all the other tabloid crap. Well, not as far as I know anyway. Norway v Scotland came on the TV, which was just inside the open window of the bar, so we watched bits of that.

Jon went off to phone Helen and she came down shortly after 6 p.m. She looked well and seemed to be enjoying herself, and we told her about events in Marseilles, including how I'd lost my voice after two days of singing. We then went off to the campsite, in Helen's car and a taxi, and Helen told us that one of our mates was working there for Eurocamp – Nooney! We knew he'd gone to France to work on a campsite, but it could have been any of over a hundred, but he ends up at the one we stay at. Small fucking world! We checked in at the campsite and met Nooney, who looked nearly as shocked as we were. Helen showed us to our pitch, and then said she'd meet us later in the bar. We pitched three tents on one site, which took ages because the ground was rock hard, and we were all a bit clueless with tents anyway. Once they were up, I got my Darlo flag and tied it to the trees, and then Mel put his flag up next to it, as the Dutch next door looked on with bemusement. Us English always love to show everyone that we're English when we go abroad. Mind you, the Dutch had put some of their orange Holland flags next to their camper van, so we were just entering into the spirit of things. I said to one of the Dutch 'I speak a little Dutch' (in Dutch which impressed the others), and he said, 'Then we'll have to watch it.' Mel didn't hear what I said and thought I'd shouted abuse at them.

Anyway, after trying to boost Anglo-Dutch relations, it

was time to go and get pissed at the campsite bar and disco. We got the beers in and watched the Brazil v Morocco game on a big screen. It wasn't all that interesting so we talked about football instead, mainly Darlo, Sunderland and Arsenal, our respective teams. As we got more pissed, and took the piss out of each other, Sven slapped me on top of my head, which given the severe sun burn up there was nearly as bad as a kick in the balls. My instant response was a back handed punch in the gut, which almost winded him. I didn't think I'd punched him that hard, but I think it made him realise how fucked the top of my head was.

After a few more beers we headed next door to the disco, where they were playing some good tunes to start with, so I went straight on to the dancefloor, which was surrounded by tables around the edge of the room. The other people on the dancefloor can't have been much older then eleven or twelve, which must have looked strange, a few pissed up lads dancing next to a bunch of little girls. They soon disappeared with their parents though once all six of us were up on the stage, especially with me wearing the Darlo on Tour t-shirt and sporting a sunburnt skin head. It soon filled up in there and we had a right laugh, especially when Sven fell over for no apparent reason and just lay there laughing. Jon managed to fall over as well, while dancing away and forgetting about the step down from the dancefloor behind him. The DJ played 'Vindaloo' about five times, which brought the English flocking to the dancefloor each time, going mental and singing along. 'Where on earth are you from, we're from En-g-land ... na-na na, na-na na, na-na na na-na na, na na ... we're gonna score one more than you ... England.' Fucking loved it!

By 3 a.m. most people had gone, including Mel, Sven and

Nooney, but I just kept on dancing. The DJ put on some real banging tunes and I was loving it, just like my old clubbing days when I was a student. Dancing like fuck I was, all on my own, apart from when some bird joined me for a few minutes, and then Matt and Jon for a while. Then I was fucked, so the three of us went back to the tents to crash out. Another late night in France, and yet again it was fucking brilliant! It was a good, friendly, international (but predominantly English) atmosphere on that campsite. But the next day we were off to Toulouse.

Day 5, Wednesday 17 June

I woke up with the usual hangover, and went off for a shit, shower and shave. I thought I could smell toothpaste, and when I opened my toiletries bag I realised why – the cap of the toothpaste had come off. Not just ordinary toothpaste, but the stuff combined with mouthwash and is dead runny. And the stuff covered everything in the bag. Fuck!

I got back to the tents and Nooney had decided to quit his job after just one day, and come with us to Toulouse to try and find work there. So after a bottle of water for breakfast, and feeling sick for 20 minutes, me, Matt, Mel and Nooney headed off to the reception to check out, leaving Sven and Jon who were staying there until Friday. We told them to go to the London Town pub in Toulouse when they got there. We got the receptionist to phone us a taxi, and told her we wanted to pay. She just ignored us after phoning the taxi and served someone else, so we waited outside for the taxi and left without paying.

The taxi driver was a bit of a laugh. We talked about football and I came out with my favourite French phrase of the time, *Angleterre va ganger le coup du monde* (England will win the World Cup). The taxi driver kept mentioning famous English footballers like Bobby Charlton and Gary Lineker, and then came out with the favourite phrase of the French at the time, *les hooligans anglais*. Twat!

We arrived at the station in St Raphael and waited about half an hour for the train to Marseilles, during which time Nooney put on his zombie mask that he had, which gave some Frogs on the platform a laugh. We got a compartment to ourselves on the train, so out came the walkman and speakers, and on went my World Cup special tape. Nooney said that he had a few tapes with him, but to say a few is taking the piss. He pulled out tape after tape from his rucksack, and must have had at least 40. The four of us sat there for the next hour and a half, singing along to 'Three Lions', 'This Time' and all the rest, before the train took us into Marseilles. We were back at Marseilles train station, but there were virtually no other English there, obviously most had left the day before like us. We had over an hour to wait for the train to Toulouse, so we went to McDonalds for something to eat. I was still feeling a bit rough, even though it was nearly 5 p.m. During the first few days of the holiday, my diet consisted almost entirely of beer, water, bread and burgers, and I never really ate anything until late afternoon, which probably explains why I felt like shit for most mornings and afternoons early on.

Anyway, we made our way to the train and got ourselves our own compartment, only to be moved by the conductor because all the seats were reserved in that one. So we got another compartment but had to share with some poofy looking Arab in a suit. We still put the tape on though, and to start with listened to some comedy tape that Nooney had. Some bloke was going on about the disappearance of white dog shit, which can never be seen any more. Matt's explanation was that the French nicked it all and used it to paint Marseilles. Seems about right.

The Arab bloke fucked off to another compartment, after

dropping a smelly as fuck fart. Maybe he ate all the white dog shit. We sat there for the next four hours, admiring the scenery, and listening to Nooney's and Matt's tape collections – The Rolling Stones, The Beatles, Elvis, *The Godfather* soundtrack, and even Frank Sinatra. We got to Toulouse at about 9 p.m., and found the usual welcome of loads of police at the station, although it wasn't too bad because it was still five days before the England match. It was then time to begin the search for a hotel, which was to prove to be a right fucking head do-er.

We followed a sign post to a hotel half a mile down the road, but when we got there the receptionist said they were full (*c'est complet*). Lying bastard! I was still wearing my Darlo on Tour t-shirt, and the tosser probably thought we were some of the famous English hooligans. So we headed off to the train station to try the tourist office, but it was shut. Bollocks! We headed towards the centre down a road that was full of hotels. On the way there this English bloke stopped us and said all the hotels said they were full, didn't want any English and we'd have no chance wearing England hats and t-shirts, and also we shouldn't go into the hotels as a group of four. He added that the mayor of Toulouse had declared war on English supporters, after hearing about the events in Marseilles. We were in for a good time!

So we split into twos and tried a few hotels, and at first got the same reply, *c'est complet*. But then Mel and Nooney got lucky and managed to get a room. Me and Matt went in after them, but surprise surprise, *c'est complet*. Do I look like a thug or something? Oh well, we tried a few more but got the same reply. We passed a load of South African fans having a good singsong and getting pissed, and they were having a laugh with some Danes ahead of the next day's match.

We saw this South African who we'd seen a couple of times already that day, and he said he'd ask this Dane who spoke French if he knew of anywhere. The Dane said they had somewhere in the city centre, and we could crash out there if we got stuck. He asked where we were from, and when we said Yorkshire he went on about the film *The Full Monty*. He said, 'Tonight we party and do full monty.' No thanks, mate. Didn't really fancy the idea of sleeping in a room full of Danes who like doing the full monty.

So we headed off to try some more hotels, but had the idea of Mel and Nooney wearing our rucksacks and trying the hotels. They went into one place and were there for over half an hour, so we thought they must have got us room, seeing as they didn't look quite so thuggish, plus Nooney spoke French as good as me. They came out and said there were no rooms for that night, but they'd booked two rooms for the weekend. The woman in there had been really helpful and phoned loads of hotels, and managed to get us somewhere near Le Place Capitole, the main square where the town hall is. When hearing that we're English the receptionist at the other hotel asked if we were hooligans, to which the woman replied 'no'. Just as well I never went in there.

So after hearing the good news that we'd got a room, I had a quick change in the street and put a shirt on. We found the hotel and dumped our bags off. The old bloke on reception seemed sound enough, and appreciated me speaking French. After a quick wash we then went to Pizza Hut for beer and something to eat.

The food was all right, but the service was crap and the

beer was as flat as fuck, so we left a tip of 20 centimes (2p). Matt had problems ordering a hot chocolate which a couple of locals found funny (so did we). I think the waitress thought he meant a chocolate cake or something, because she was quite surprised when he said he wanted it before the pizza. After that we sat in the square (Le Place Capitole) and watched the goings on. Some Frogs tried to sell us some weed. We said no but ended up talking to them anyway, about football, English fans, the press and Toulouse. One of them said that he was a Paris St Germain fan, and another said that they're going to the Notting Hill Carnival in London. They said that they didn't really believe what the press said about English football fans, but don't really have much else to go by. They would by the time the weekend was over. They even offered to let us stay at their flat for the next night. They seemed okay but we couldn't really trust them, so we didn't bother. Although we could have kicked them in if we had to, they could have pulled knives on us or got some of their mates to nick our bags if we'd stayed at their flat. So we stayed around for a bit and headed off back to the hotels.

As we were leaving, some English lads started talking to us, right fucking nutters they were, from Stockport and Leeds. One of them said (in a Manc accent)) 'No one's ever taken Marseilles before, Man U, Everton have been there but couldn't do it. But we fucking took Marseilles. Fair go to the Tunisians like, they had a go, but we fucking took Marseilles.' We just agreed with the mad fucker. He then went on to say how it's gonna kick off with the police in Toulouse at the weekend, and 'they've even made a square for us'. As we left, he said, 'Remember lads, you've won the first lottery of life ... you were born British.' Rather similar to what Cecil Rhodes said, 'To be born English is to win the lottery of life'. Too fucking right!

Mel and Nooney saw them again later as they were going to their hotel. The same one was asking these Frogs, 'Where's the fucking train station? Train station? *Gare? Gaaarre?'* Thick twat! But I wouldn't complain if they were with us in a fight. Anyway, we got to the hotel, my turn to have the bed, and I fell asleep, not pissed for the first time in nearly a week.

Day 6, Thursday 18 June

I woke up without a hangover, which was a new experience. I thought we'd missed breakfast, 'cos it was gone half past ten by the time we left the room, but after asking they said they'll do us a breakfast. So we sat down and had bread, coffee and orange juice. On they way out, a reporter from the *Daily Express* started talking to us. He was a right twat. Asking crap like 'Did you see the trouble in Marseilles? Do you know the movements of the hooligans? Have you seen any trouble in Toulouse?' and other similar crap. Given how much the press had slagged us off, I would have hit the cunt if we weren't stood in the reception in view of a few staff and other guests, but he would have only made up some shit story about being savagely attacked by a football hooligan in a hotel. So I told him the press had exaggerated what happened in Marseilles, which he denied, and because of all the shite in the media it's difficult to find accommodation in Toulouse if you're English. I told him about our night of singing in Marseilles, when we had a laugh with the locals, but he didn't want to know, just kept asking stupid questions about the hooligans. I said it helps if you speak French, which he didn't, and after speaking to the receptionist (in French) who confirmed that they'd no rooms for that night, me and Matt headed off to Mel and Nooney's hotel, up near the station. It's thick twats like that reporter that give England a bad name with all their sensationalist misinterpretation and bullshit stories, not us, being patriotic and having a laugh while trying to speak the local lingo.

We got to the hotel and met the other two, before going to the train station to dump our bags off in the lockers. The plan was to head down to the stadium and buy tickets down there for the day's match, South Africa v Denmark, but a Dane in the station asked us if we wanted to buy tickets. He wanted 700 francs each (£70), but we got him down to 550 francs, which wasn't too bad. Nooney didn't get one though, because he decided to spend the day looking for a job.

We decided to go for a drink and left the station. Just outside the station, we bumped into Hollis who was one of the lads in the bar in Marseilles (the Wolves fan). 'Alright Darlo,' he said. He'd managed to get in one of the Formula 1 hotels near the airport, which was part of the same hotel chain as the one he stayed at in Marseilles. His mates weren't coming over until the weekend, so he came with us and decided to go to the match.

The five of us went for a drink, and I was feeling a bit rough again, despite only one beer during the previous night. I soon felt better though, and we headed off towards the stadium, while Nooney left us to go and look for work. We arranged to meet him at the station at 9 p.m. It was another hot day in the south of France, and I borrowed Hollis's sunhat to stop my head burning. We got down to the river where there were boats taking people down to the stadium, so we paid our 15 francs and got on a boat which was full of South Africans.

Although I wasn't too bothered about the result of the match, and expected Denmark to win, I was supporting South Africa because I've got loads of cousins over there.

40

I've not yet been to South Africa, but I've met a few of my cousins who've come over to England in the last few years. So I was doing my bit for the family and supporting 'Bafana Bafana', which is what the fans call the team. I think it means 'the boys' or something.

The South Africans on the boat were a right good laugh, singing away. At one point they sang 'If you think Schmeichel's a wanker clap your hands', which we just had to join in with. They also kept singing this brilliant song that we'd heard them singing the night before, though I haven't a clue what the words were. I was later told that it's an old miners song that they sing to encourage the team to work hard, and it's called *Shosholoza*. This tall bloke who was wearing a South African football shirt then got up and put on his Nelson Mandela mask, got hold of the microphone and did a Nelson-style speech – 'Friends ... thank you for being here today...' It was well funny.

When the boat pulled up, the police were checking that everyone had match tickets. Hollis didn't have a ticket at that point, so Matt put his ticket from Marseilles in among the three that we'd bought at the station, and the copper let us all through. There weren't any ticket touts around there for Hollis, so we followed the road up to the stadium, and went down to the area outside the turnstiles. There was an area of shade down there underneath the road we'd just walked along, so we stood down there to get out of the boiling heat. Toulouse was just as hot as Marseilles – we'd forgotten that it was just as far south.

There was some sort of World Cup band playing all sorts of jazzy samba music, which a few South Africans were dancing to. Hollis decided to head back down to near where we got off the boat, so we said if we didn't see him later we'd meet up at the station at midday on the next day, outside the World Cup information office. Just before he left, I bought a 'South Africa – Coupe du Monde 98' baseball cap for 150 francs. A lot of money for a hat but I needed it to keep the sun off my head, and I wanted to show my support for South Africa. We also had the idea that wearing a South Africa hat might make getting a hotel easier later on.

After listening to the samba band for a while and chilling out in the shade, me, Mel and Matt went through the turnstiles, facing the usual ticket check and police body search. They didn't say a word about the Danish name on our tickets, just a quick look for the watermark. What was the government going on about with those stupid adverts before the tournament started? 'All tickets have the purchaser's name printed on them'. So fucking what! All those adverts did was waste taxpayers' money, as if they don't do that enough. No one payed a blind bit of notice to that crappy government information film, and we were justified in not doing so, other than often getting ripped off.

Anyway, after taking a quick photo of the three of us outside the stadium, we walked around to the appropriate entrance and went inside to take our seats. It was still ages until kick off, but we wanted to get a good place for Mel's flag, a three and a half yard white ensign with Darlington sewn across the centre and also on the Union Jack in the corner. We found a good place for the flag, tied over a high wall in front of all the seats, quite near to the corner flag. Mel said that it should be seen on TV every time someone took a corner from that end, especially as the TV cameras were on the opposite side of the ground to us. It turned out that loads of people saw the flag back home, so now Darlington are world famous.

Our seats were right next to the fence separating the Danish fans from the neutral section, and soon the place was full of Danes. There was a Scottish flag in the same end, but not nearly as big as the Darlo flag, and there was also a Mexican flag. There was also a group of South Africans in the same section, but other than that it was all Danish. They were a good friendly bunch of fans, enjoying the party atmosphere of the World Cup, but I would rather have been down the other end with the fellow countrymen of my cousins. One bloke a few rows in front, who was obviously pissed out of his head, stood on his seat and dropped his shorts, and waved his cock around for everyone to see. The steward told him to stop after about five minutes, but that's all. If he had been English, no doubt the riot police would have dragged him out.

Once the match started it looked like Denmark would win easily, especially when they scored after eight minutes. The Danes went mental, and being a semi-neutral, I stood up and applauded with the rest of them. South Africa managed to get back into the game though, and were unlucky not to score before half-time.

I got talking to the Dane next to me, saying that I was English. He asked why I was wearing a South Africa hat, and I told him it was to keep the sun off my head, and also because of my family over there. He said he supported some small club called Vram in the Danish second division, and I told him of my allegiance to the mighty Darlo. So we both proudly support relatively obscure teams.

Once the second half started, South Africa began creating a few decent chances, and the game became quite open on the whole. After Alan Nielsen nearly scored, the Danes all chanted his name, and the bloke next to me that I'd been talking to said, 'You can sing this too.' So I did.

But then South Africa scored! So I jumped up and cheered, although I didn't go mental like when England or Darlo score. After that, South Africa were unlucky not to win the game, but then the referee completely spoilt the game, by sending off three players for minor offences. I don't think any of them were worthy of a sending off. Apparently, Michel Platini, great player in his time but now a complete twat as vice-president of the French Organising Committee, had told referees that they'd been too soft on players and should apply the rules more strictly. The result? Three send-ings off in this game and one or two in the other one played that day. Cheers Michel (and the ref), for fucking up a good game of football, you twat!

So the game ended 1–1, and I was happy that South Africa got a point and scored their first-ever World Cup goal. The atmosphere around that game was totally different to England games, with a very low police presence, not like the masses of riot police that you get for England. The three of us then left the stadium and went back down to the river to get another boat. This one was mainly full of Danes, French, English and Scottish. The Jocks started whistling the 'Flower of Scotland', so I replied with 'God Save the Queen'. They must have thought it was strange coming from some-one wearing a South Africa hat.

We walked up back into the city centre, and began trying hotels for a room for the night. The first few were full (even for South Africans), but we then found a place that had a few rooms for the night, just down from the Place Capitole/Place Wilson and the hotel that we'd booked for the weekend. We booked a couple of rooms, but thought that Nooney might have booked us in somewhere, in between doing his job hunting. We told the hotel manager that we'd be back within an hour if we wanted the room, which he said he was okay with, although I took the hotel's phone number anyway.

So the three of us went up to the station, and on the way got talking to a black South African family about the match. I said that I'd got cousins over there but have never been over, and she said I must go to South Africa. Too fucking right, I thought. It was her who told me all about that song I mentioned earlier, the old miner's song. They were sound, nice and cheerful, just glad to be at the World Cup, not too bothered about results. All that's missing from the latter stages of the World Cup, once these lesser nations in footballing terms are out.

We soon got to the station and met Nooney, who was pissed off because he couldn't find work, and had decided to get a flight home that night 'cos he was skint, apart from enough for the flight home. We persuaded him to stay for the night though, especially as we'd got him a room in the hotel. So he agreed to stay, and after getting our bags from the lockers and a quick phone call to confirm our booking at the hotel, we went down there to check in.

We dumped our bags off and then went out to get some food and beer, choosing to go to a Chinese place near the hotel we'd got for the weekend. The place was called A Dong, and we went inside and got ourselves a table. We asked the waiter if they had the football on (France v Saudi Arabia), and he moved us to a quieter part of the restaurant with a TV right next to us.

The four of us all had the Menu a Dong, which was basically a choice of things for 65 francs. After ordering, the waiter brought us some kind of Chinese aperitif to drink.

I dunno what it what was but it was fucking nice. Soon necked it down. And then necked my beer. Time for another one. Our starters arrived and we all got stuck in. One problem though. No forks, just chopsticks, which I'd never previously managed to eat with before. Oh well, when in France, do as the Chinese do. I just about managed to eat the spring rolls with the chopsticks, with a little help from my fingers, but then I made a big mistake. The waiter had brought us a small dish of chilli sauce. 'This is very hot,' he said. 'Sound,' I said, 'I love chilli.' So I put loads of it on my spring rolls. When I tasted it, my mouth was hotter than a vindaloo cooked in a furnace! Aaaaaarrrrhhhhh! Hot as fuck! No, hotter. But I still ate it all, I couldn't let a bit of chilli sauce get the better of me. My mouth was burning like fuck though, especially the sore I'd got on my lips. Loads of water, loads of beer, more water, more beers, and I was just about back to normal.

Then the main course came (after more beer). I had some sort of chicken curry with fried rice, and it was lovely. Not hot enough though, so being a bit of a masochistic bastard I had loads more of the chilli sauce and mixed it in with the curry. That was better, can't beat having your mouth on fire when eating out!

Another beer, another course, this time the ice-cream for dessert. We ate that, watched the rest of the football, which France won 4–0, and then talked to a couple of the staff for a while. They were quite sound, and we talked about football, and when Nooney mentioned that he was looking for a job they said that he'd be better off trying a few coastal resorts. After paying the bill, we left the Chinese and headed for the Place Capitole.

There was loads of locals driving down to the square,

continuously beeping their horns, celebrating their win at football in the irritating way that Continentals do. It got worse around the square itself, they were making a right fucking noise. 'You'd think they've just won the World Cup Final, not just beaten Saudi Arabia,' I said.

The Place Capitole was mainly a mixture of French, Danish and South Africans, partying away the night, with a few English like us saving ourselves for the weekend when we'd take over the whole square. We sat around near where we were on the previous night, but soon got bored and went back to the hotel. So day six was over, we'd been to another World Cup match, and although I'd had a few beers, I wasn't anything like I was in Marseilles, Fréjus or Calais. Which meant I couldn't sleep for ages, 'cos it was still hot as fuck, even at 1 a.m., the hotel was a bit scummy, and I wasn't pissed enough to just pass out. Soon dozed off though.

Day 7, Friday 19 June

I woke up without a particularly bad head, for the second day running. The weirdest thing about the hotel was that the bathroom had a shower, a sink and a bidet, but no fucking bog! Daft bastards! So I went out of our door, wearing nothing but undies and a t-shirt, and there's a room full of South Africans in front of me having breakfast. D'oh! Quick retreat back into the room, put my jeans on, and then went for a crap, into a toilet that opens directly on to the dining room. Sat there, had a crap, flushed the chain, opened the door expecting loads of people to be looking at me after eating their breakfast, but they'd all gone. I didn't think I'd made that much noise on the bog.

Anyway I got my bag packed and we all had breakfast. The usual crap, bread, coffee, orange and more bread. Mel told us he'd had a cockroach land on him when he was in the shower, so the hotel was instantly renamed from Hotel Francois 1st to Hotel Cockroach.

After leaving that place we went back up to the station. Nooney phoned the airport and got booked on a flight to London that left an hour later, so he left to get a train to the airport. He'd only left home a week earlier, expecting to be in France for the summer, but met us, quit his job and went home before us. He'd had a good few days though.

After Nooney left we dumped our bags in the lockers

again, and then went to meet Hollis, who turned up shortly afterwards. I went to the bog at the station while we were waiting for Hollis. When I got there, there was a woman sat there with a price list – 20 francs for a piss, 30 francs for a shit, and 50 francs for a shower. There was even a little turnstile to walk through.

After a few beers at a café opposite the station, the four of us went down to McDonalds at the Place Capitole, got some food and went to the Place Wilson, which was just next to it, scoffed our food and sat on the grass all afternoon. It was quite relaxing there, sat in the shade admiring all the French women walking past. Some of them were fucking gorgeous, must be something they put in the water in Toulouse. Although there is a large student population there, so that probably has something to do with it.

Hollis looked like your typical Englishman abroad. Short hair, intermittently covered with an England sunhat, beer belly in full sight, shorts, Union Jack towel. Mind you, I can't have looked much better. Even though I was still wearing the South Africa hat, I'm sure most people realised we were all English. It was sound sat there though, chilling out, dozing off, admiring the scenery.

By late afternoon though, we decided to go and check in at the Hotel Trianon Wilson, where we'd booked into the other night, and Hollis went off back to his hotel. He said his mates were arriving tomorrow, but we said we'd probably see him around in the square (Place Capitole). So the three of us went to check in, and just crashed out for a few hours in the hotel room, 'cos it was just too hot outside.

We asked the manager if he had any more rooms for the weekend, for Sven and Jon who were arriving that evening. He said he had, so we booked a room for the two of them, and went up to the station to get our bags and meet the other two. We got our bags, waited for the train from Marseilles, but they weren't on it. Fuck! When I got back home and saw Jon at work, he said they'd arrived at half past nine, and we'd left at ten past nine, so we only just missed them. Oh well, the three of us went back to the hotel, which was much better than the Hotel Cockroach, cancelled the other room, dumped our bags off, and then went in search of the London Town pub that was in the guide book.

I had a quick look at the map of Toulouse that was in a city guide book, and thought I knew what direction to go in. We went through the main square and down a small street, looking out for an English pub. Couldn't find it though! We'd gone in completely the wrong direction, and ended up miles out of the way, and were walking around a really quiet area of the city. We went into a café to ask for directions and have a drink, but the owner was a complete twat. He made us feel like scum, saying that they'd stopped serving food and we couldn't have a drink on its own. He obviously didn't want any young English lads in there, and I could've chinned the cunt, but that would have only made things worse. But his waiter, who'd lived in England and sounded more Dutch than French, was quite helpful and gave us directions.

So we walked back up to the Place Capitole, buying a can of beer each on the way, took the right turning this time, walked down another small street and found the London Town pub five minutes later. At last! We'd found the English pub. We went in and it wasn't particularly busy, but there was mainly English in there and the staff were welcoming, and we spent the next few hours drinking pints and not half litres, or anything, getting slowly pissed and talking to a

50

few others in there. And of course, they had 'Vindaloo' and 'Three Lions' on the juke box. It was definitely the place to go for the next two nights, as all the other English would be arriving over the weekend, ready for the Romania match on the Monday. So after a night in an English pub, and feeling more pissed than the previous two nights, we went back to the hotel and crashed out, safe in the knowledge that we'd got a decent hotel for the weekend and had found the London Town pub. Roll on Saturday night!

May 8, Saturday 20 June

I woke up late, Matt went out for a walk about, and then I went out for some breakfast. Me and Mel went to the sandwich shop around the corner, and then back to the hotel. I had one of those *croque monsieurs*, which is basically a cheese and ham toastie, but fucking lovely. I soon got bored of watching Eurosport in the hotel room, so I went out to buy some postcards. I walked up the road in the warm sun, and found a shop selling postcards and other stuff. I noticed an England baseball cap among a load of World Cup souvenirs, so I couldn't resist it. I ended up spending 160 francs on the hat, 14 postcards and stamps. Walking back to the hotel, I could notice the difference in looks I was getting from the French. I'd walked up there wearing the South Africa hat, and back wearing the England hat. They were probably thinking, *Ooh la la, c'est un hooligan anglais*. But I didn't give a toss what they were thinking. I was feeling proud to show the world (well, Toulouse) that I was one of the lucky ones to be born English.

Back in the hotel, I wrote a few postcards but soon got bored so I crashed out for a bit. As I was sat writing the postcards, I had live entertainment from outside, courtesy of a load of English at the pub around the corner (The Melting Pot), singing 'No Surrender', 'Rule Britannia' and all the rest ('Rule Britannia, Britannia rules the waves,

Britons never never never shall be slaves...'). Saturday afternoon was fairly uneventful really. Mel was asleep in his room, Matt was watching Eurosport and writing his diary, and I was dozing and writing the odd postcard. But by 7 p.m., it was time to go out and get pissed. The three of us headed down to the Place Capitole, and there was a few more English around than before. We went straight to the London Town pub, cutting out the two-mile detour of the previous night, and showing a group of other English the way there. When we got there the place was packed, with a few people stood outside and loads of singing inside. We were certainly in for a good night.

'Three Lions' and then 'Vindaloo' were blaring out of the juke box, with the whole pub singing along, probably about 80-odd people all together. It was a great laugh, singing 'Rule Britannia', 'No Surrender', and the old classic (to the tune of 'She'll be coming 'round the mountain when she comes': 'Would you like your chicken supper Bobby Sands, would you like your chicken supper Bobby Sands, would you like your chicken supper, you dirty Fenian fucker, would you like your chicken supper Bobby Sands?' This of course referred to the IRA hunger striker who smeared his cell with his own shit and starved himself to death in the early 1980s. We decided to get some food and return afterwards and, as we walked out of the pub, a familiar song started up: 'Who do you think you are kidding Mister Hitler, if you think we're on the run? We are the boys who will stop your little game, we are the boys who will make you think again. So who do you think you are kidding Mister Hitler, if you think old England's done?' which is the theme tune to *Dad's Army*, to those who haven't lived. We'd definitely be back shortly, after that little singsong.

We reluctantly left the pub and went off to find a café. None of us had eaten since the morning, and we needed a beer base. We found a decent place down the road, with a mixture of English and French, families and football fans. We sat outside to start with, but the wind kept blowing everything all over the place, so we sat just inside. Got the beers in (Mel had red wine again), and I had an absolutely gorgeous pizza. Better than the wafer thin effort in Marseilles anyway. So after a sound meal we went back to the London Town pub, via a cash machine (thank fuck my cash card is a Visa and not Switch). We basically carried on as before, getting pissed, singing away with the rest of the pub. One chant of 'Barmy Army' went on for about ten minutes. Later on, someone started singing 'Shadwell Army', from the film *I.D.*, which is about four coppers who go undercover to infiltrate a gang of football hooligans (to use tabloid terms) but one of them loves it and becomes one of them, getting stuck in whenever he can. Good film. Anyway, the whole pub joined in with the chant.

It was a right laugh in that place, with people standing up on the bar or a table, getting everyone to shut up, with a few people going 'sssshhhh ... speech', which would be followed by 'na-na na' or 'Glenn Hoddle's Barmy Army', and the place would go mental again. But, at 11 p.m. the staff said they had to close the bar, because the police said that all bars must close at 11 p.m. instead of the usual 2 p.m. over the weekend, because we're English and we're all hooligans. Which is pure fucking discrimination in my opinion. But I'd had plenty of beer, and was ready to go to the square and see what was happening, so chants of 'going to the square, going to the square, na-na na na, na-na na na' went around the pub. After a quick conga of about 50 people went out and back in the pub a couple of times, we all went down to the Place Capitole, singing all the way, and doing the conga for most of the way.

When we got near the square, we all started singing 'En-g-land, En-g-land, En-g-land...', and all the English in the square seemed to flock towards us. So there we were, about 200 English, pissed and merry, stood in the square with about a dozen camera crews around, who were obviously looking to film trouble. But we all started singing, especially 'Barmy Army' and 'Let's Go Fucking Mental, Let's Go Fucking Mental, Na-na na na, na-na na na'. Then it was 'Sit Down, If You Love England', so all 200 of us sat down on the ground, and then the song became 'Stand Up, If You Hate the Press', and we all stood up. Funny as fuck! The TV crews, locals and non-English tourists looked on with much bemusement. I then had the idea of singing *Dambusters*, and about 20 seconds later, all of us were walking around the square, arms out to the sides, singing the *Dambusters* theme tune. What a sight!

After trying to get everyone in the middle of the square by singing 'Let's go to the middle', etc, we went over to McDonalds which was still open, seeing as most people had fucked up their voices and it all went quiet for a bit. As we were in the queue, two of the fern trees next to us suddenly opened up, a familiar face appears and says (in a broad West Midlands accent), 'I'm the guardian of these trees'. Hollis! Pissed out of his head. 'Alright Darlo'. So we got a beer from McDonalds, stood around talking to Hollis and his mates who had arrived that day, and then it was time to head back to the hotel and crash out. What a great night that was.

Day 9, Sunday 21 June

Sunday began with another lie in, and then the three of us went for breakfast. We decided to go to the Chinese fast food take away, seeing as it was cheap. I ended up having some sort of fried crab and spring rolls for breakfast. Made a change from French bread anyway.

We sat in the Place Wilson again and scoffed our breakfast, before heading off to the Place Capitole, where we'd been singing the night before. There were loads more English around, and the England Supporters Band (a bunch of Sheffield Wednesday fans who'd just released a recording of 'The Great Escape') were playing tunes in the middle of the square.

We saw Hollis and his mates sitting on the wall, and we all spent the early part of the afternoon in the sun, drinking beer, watching people play football, and listening (and singing along to) 'The Great Escape'. After a while though, me, Matt and Mel went back to the hotel to crash out for a bit, seeing as it was so hot outside. We watched the afternoon's football which was Germany v Yugoslavia. The Germans were losing 2–0 at one point, but true to form they managed to draw 2–2. Lucky bastards!

I managed to get my postcards finished, and then fell asleep watching more football on the TV. Matt woke me up as the football finished, and the three of us went out for another night of beer and singing in the London Town pub, although my head was a bit fucked after my little sleep. Talking of my head, the sunburn on top had began to peel nicely, and left a funny pattern in my hair where the dead skin was clumped together, and it looked sort of like a tortoiseshell. Lovely! No wonder I always wore my hat for the rest of the holiday.

When we got to the London Town pub it was just as packed as the night before, with quite a few people outside and loads inside, singing away. So just like the night before, we got the beers in and had a good sing-song, with 'Vindaloo' and 'Three Lions' on the juke box, and everyone singing 'Barmy Army' and 'No Surrender', plus all the other favourites.

We stood outside for a bit, talked to a Tottenham fan with a fucking huge nose, true to style for a Yid, a West Ham fan, a couple of Leeds fans, and a Coventry fan who showed us his stab wound from Marseilles, a fucking great hole in his upper arm. As we were stood there an old bloke pulled up opposite us in his car, accompanied by a decent looking girl. This prompted shouts of 'Nicole, Nicole' and 'Papa' as in the Renault adverts. Everyone was laughing like fuck, including the old Frenchman, although the girl (presumably his granddaughter) seemed a bit embarrassed by it all. But then we got hungry, so we set off in the search for food again, heading towards the restaurant we'd gone to the previous night.

When we got there though it was closed, and there were a few coppers hanging around. There was more of a tense atmosphere than the previous night with all that lot around, obviously expecting trouble of some sort. We found a small café just around the corner with a few English outside, and decided to go in there. It was more like an English café, with the menu consisting of sandwiches, beer, and an English breakfast. Fucking yes! A fry up. English breakfast at 9 p.m. Sorted.

So the three of us sat there drinking beer, and then scoffed our bacon, eggs, beans, mushrooms, cooked tomatoes and toast. What a treat! We noticed a couple of English reporters sitting down just before we left, so we sat there taking the piss out of tabloid papers (two had been left on our table by the previous people). I just kept saying stuff like 'people who work for tabloids must be thick as fuck', and 'the tabloids are a disgrace to our country after what they've said about us'. The reporters never reacted though, probably too shit scared, or too thick to realise we were taking the piss out of them. So we paid the bill, but not before I got a picture of me and the waitress. She was gorgeous! Your typical French sexy chic, who didn't speak much English and couldn't stop smiling. Nice!

After that it was back to the London Town pub, but surprisingly it was fairly quiet in there. Most people must have gone off down to the square, but we stayed there until closing time and then went back to the square. When we got there, there were loads of people over by McDonalds having a singsong, and leaning into passing cars to beep the horn. Sound! Another mad night in le Place Capitole.

This time we had a couple of cameras, so we got loads of photos of everyone going mental. It was a right laugh, singing 'Barmy Army' and all the rest. We saw Hollis & Co again, who were just as pissed as the previous night. At one point some lass got on a bloke's shoulders, and a rendition of 'Get your tits out for the lads' went up, followed by 'Tits out, for the En-g-land' to the tune of 'you're shit and you know you are' or 'Go West'. She was well embarrassed. The singing went on for ages, and at one point we sang 'We're on the march with Hoddle's army, we're all going to Saint Denis, and we'll really shake 'em up, when we win the World Cup, 'cos England are the greatest football team'. We were filled with such optimism and high spirits that night. The World Cup was ours.

After an hour or so the singing moved over to the middle of the square, and then died down, so we eventually headed off back to the hotel. Those two nights in the square were one of the many highlights of the World Cup. Fucking mental! It was a brilliant atmosphere in Toulouse, which I have to say was my favourite World Cup venue. But there's no way that the press would have reported any of the party atmosphere of Toulouse, they're just interested in the sort of crap that happened in Marseilles, where they can continue to label all English football fans as mindless scum. Why are the media so pessimistic and sensationalist? Can't they report something positive about us for once? But I'm not letting the media wankers take away my good impressions of Toulouse.

Day 10, Monday 22 June

After our last night at the best hotel so far, the Trianon Wilson, and another lie in, the three of us went up to dump our bags at the station. We didn't have tickets for the England v Romania game, and we were going to just watch it in a bar, but we decided that we'd try and buy tickets outside. We didn't expect to get any though, because we weren't going to pay more than £50–£60, so we were booked on to the 11.15 p.m. overnight train to Paris.

We got up to the station and found that the lockers were all full, but we found another place to leave luggage next to the bus station, which had much more room. After queuing up with another 30-odd English, we dumped our bags and went off back towards the Place Capitole, stopping for breakfast on the way. We stopped off at the Melting Pot pub after something to eat, and saw Jon from the train to Marseilles at the pub next door, so we had a chat with him and his mate for a bit. There were also a few Middlesbrough fans at the Melting Pot with a huge Boro flag tied up on the window.

There were loads more people around than the previous day, which wasn't surprising considering it was match day. On the way there, I heard a familiar tune coming out of a car. I looked around and an English car was going past, with 'There'll always be an England' blasting out for all to hear.

Day 10, Monday 22 June

Just what was needed. The square itself was a real sight – just about every single window of the Town Hall, plus the other non-commercial buildings to the side and opposite, were covered in English flags. It looked sound as fuck! St George's flags, Union Jacks, White Ensigns, Red Ensigns, even an Ulster flag, from all over England. Didn't see any Darlo flags, and we'd left ours in our bags at the station. We did see an England flag with 'Bollocks' written across it though.

We stayed around there for a bit and joined in some of the singing, which was mainly around the cafés opposite the Town Hall. I was disgusted by what I saw next. Two separate things in fact. First, some twat had a Cardiff City Welsh flag, and was wearing a Cardiff City shirt. I know Wales are so shit and never get to the World Cup themselves, but that's no excuse for a Cardiff wanker to join our party. After the amount that they slag us off as well. The fucking cheek of it. If I'd seen him at night without the cameras around and a few beers inside me, I might have kicked the fuck out of the Welsh cunt, after what had happened to me down at their place a few weeks earlier.

But then, as I looked the other way in disgust at the Welsh scum, what did I see? A fucking Hartlepool fan! The second one I'd seen in France! The monkey-hanging scum bastard! For those that don't know why scum from Hartlepool are called monkey-hangers: apparently, in the Napoleonic Wars, a French warship was ship wrecked off the coast of Hartlepool, and all of the crew died, leaving only a small pet monkey alive. In those days it was French military tradition to dress pet monkeys in military uniform. Now the people of Hartlepool had never seen a Frenchman before, nor a monkey for that matter, so they accused it of being a spy. So they had a trial for it, found it guilty and hung the fucker. And to this day, the thick scum bastards from that shit town are still called the monkey-hangers, especially those wankers that associate themselves with the shit football team that have never won anything (Darlo have), have never been to Wembley (Darlo have), usually finish below Darlo, and consistently get lower attendances than Darlo. So there! The scum bastards probably shared the same shirt as the club could only afford to make one. But I have to admit, there is one good thing about Hartlepool – they're not Welsh.

Anyway, enough slagging off the scum of the Third Division. There were some great sights in the square that afternoon, as well as all of the flags. Especially a white London cab that drove past, with the cross of St George painted over it. As we were stood around, I recognised someone. I couldn't believe it. It was the bloke from the Channel Four documentary in 1992 called *Wake up England*, all about the England fans at Sweden 92. I'd taped the programme at the time, and have watched it so many times, that I couldn't fail to recognise this bloke. He was in his forties, and on the film was talking about some trouble around a beer tent, saying 'police over-reacted 110 per cent' (in a deep Mancunian accent). So I went up to him and said, Oi mate', to which he replied, 'All right bud', and I said, 'Were you in that Sweden 92 video?' to which he replied, 'Aye, I were bloody plastered at the time.' I think he was pissed then as well.

Anyway, after hanging around in the square for a while, we decided to make our way towards the stadium, even though it was about another six hours until kick off. We followed the river down towards the stadium, stopping for a can of beer along the way. As we got nearer to the stadium, we followed a quiet footpath next to the river, and sat down for a bit for a rest. A bloke walked past and we asked him if he was selling tickets. He was, but was asking 2,000 francs, which we weren't going to pay, and he headed off back the way that we'd come. We should have waited around down there for another tout and done him over for his tickets, 'cos no one would have seen us. But rather than have the police looking for us, we went down to as near to the stadium as we could get, where there was a line of police blocking the road across the bridge, not letting anyone past without tickets.

So there we were, half a mile from the stadium, with another four or five hours until kick off, with no tickets. There were quite a few people around looking for tickets, but only a few people selling and all asking stupid prices. We thought that prices might go right down just before kick off, so we headed off and went into a bar for a quick beer. After that we went down the road and found another bar around the corner, and stayed there for another couple of hours, drinking beer and having a cheese sandwich for dinner.

As kick off time got nearer, we went back up to the stadium, and asked loads of people if they were selling tickets. Most were looking for some themselves, and those that were selling were still asking stupid prices (£200+). So we ended up sat near to the police line, talking to a family that we'd seen earlier who were also looking for tickets. They were from Nottingham, the father had a ticket, but his wife and two young girls didn't.

It did our heads in sitting there, especially when coach loads of corporate ticket holders walked past, all wearing their Carlsberg t-shirts or whatever. Bastards! As if they've followed their teams all over the country, which we made a point of saying as they walked past. It seems that if you wanted a World Cup ticket, don't follow your team all over the country, just work for one of the big sponsors like Carlsberg or Snickers. As we were sat there, Emlyn Hughes and Lee Chapman walked past with all the wankers with the free tickets. We knew before going down there that we wouldn't have much chance of getting a ticket, but seeing them twats walk in with their free tickets, wearing poncey suits or free t-shirts, just made us feel resentful.

So we fucked off for another walk down the road, looking for tickets, asking just about anyone. No luck, but then Mel spotted Echo and the Bunnymen, who'd sung England's World Cup song, 'On Top of the World'. We started talking to them for a bit, about the match and their song that they'd done with the Spice Girls and others, and Ian Maculloch said how much he liked Mel B's arse. Something to tell everyone back home.

When we left them, Mel got the luck of his life. We were standing around in front of the police line, looking pissed off, when a bloke goes up to him and says, 'You want a ticket?' Mel replied, 'Yeah, how much?' and the bloke just said 'For free', shoved a ticket in Mel's hand and walked off! One ticket for England v Romania, in the Romanian end, but free! The fucker!

He could have sold it and made a small fortune, but he did the right thing and decided to go and watch the match. Me and Matt said we would have done the same. So after another look around for tickets, which was unsuccessful, Mel ran across the bridge to get to the match with just a few minutes spare. The fucker! Me and Matt hung around for a bit, with still another hundred or so others hanging around, and listened to the England fans in the stadium bellowing out 'God Save the Queen', singing along with them.

We gave up looking for tickets, and headed for the pub. On the way there, some English bloke was having a go at some foreign twat who'd sold him a ticket. The tout had taken the money and then ripped off half the ticket and kept it, so the English bloke was going to kick the fuck out of him. The tout was shitting it, jumping all over the place, but a crowd of English had gathered around, including us, and he was going nowhere. But then about a dozen riot police came over, and it was a case of 'fuck this, it's not our argument' and we moved out of the way.

So me and Matt walked down to the bar that we'd been in earlier, talking to the woman from Nottingham with her two kids, who'd not managed to get tickets. I think they were just going to wait in their car around the corner for her husband to return from the match. We got talking to a couple of others who'd also not managed to get tickets, and arrived at the bar to watch the match.

It was quite full in there and there was only one TV, so after getting a beer I ended up in the doorway, leaning forward to get a shit view of the TV. The first half was a bit crap, and it was a shite atmosphere in that pub, full of middle-aged family stand type people, so we asked the barman to order us a taxi for half-time. At half-time we stood outside and waited for the taxi, and two Leeds fans joined us, saying they wanted to go up into the town centre as well, seeing as it was so shit in there. We stood there for ages but the taxi never turned up, and one of the Leeds fans tried waving down every single vehicle that went past, even coppers. Just then some twat wearing an Inter Milan shirt jumped out of the pub and cheered. I looked at the TV and fucking Romania had scored. I should have hit the twat in the Milan shirt, but couldn't really be arsed causing a scene.

So the four of us started walking down the road in search of a taxi. The two Leeds fans left us and went to an Irish pub to watch the match, but we continued our search for a taxi, because our train left about half an hour after the match finished. Some mad black bloke was arguing with his mate, shouting some crap in French and booted a parked car. I thought he was gonna start on us at one point, but he never, and we finally found a taxi that stopped for us.

So me and Matt got dropped off outside a bar just down from the station, and went inside to watch the match with about 25 other English. At last! I could stand drinking beer and get a good view of the match. It was tense as fuck, and England were still playing a bit shite, although I have to say that Romania played quite well. But then on came Michael Owen, and scored within a few minutes. Yyyeeeeeaaaasss! We went fucking mental! Time for another beer. As we were getting used to the idea of a draw, which would have been okay, Owen nearly scores again, this time hitting the post. If only he'd been on from the start. But then, after a cock up by Le Saux and Seaman, some twat of a Romanian nips in and scores a shit goal right at the end, and that was it. Fuckers! Absolute fucking bastards! Looks like we were going to finish second in the group and go to St Etienne to play the Argies, barring a miracle, but even that wasn't guaranteed.

So, feeling pissed off to fuck, we went up to the station and got our bags, with me carrying Mel's as well. We'd told him we'd wait for him no matter what, and we'd get the

6 a.m. train if we had to, because the only other train after 11.15 was fully booked. But then he suddenly appeared, looking fucked. He'd left the match 15 minutes from the end, ran three miles, heard a cheer as he passed a pub (1–1), and couldn't believe it when we said it finished 1–2.

So the three of us were ready and on our way to Paris, where we'd planned to stay for three days and watch a couple of matches, as well as see the sights. We got on the train and found our compartment, which was a sleeper, and dumped our bags in there. There were three beds stacked up on either side, and it was all a bit cramped, but better than nothing.

We stood at the end of the carriage for a bit to smoke tabs, and got talking to some others. Then some twat Manchester City fan starts going on one. He never had a go at anyone (apart from a black porter) but kept coming out with stuff like, 'Why the fuck was Anderton playing, it's the fucking Tottenham connection, fucking Hoddle', and when we said we knew what he meant, he said, 'No, ya don't, it's fucking Tottenham', and just kept repeating himself. Tosser! Someone said 'That's one of England's top boys,' but you could've fooled me. He asked who we supported and when Matt said Arsenal he replied 'glory hunter' or some shit, which Matt certainly isn't, considering he lives a couple of miles from the ground and goes to loads of matches. When I said I support Darlington, he said, 'I used to share a cell in prison with someone from there.' Then I said I actually lived nearer to Northallerton and he said, 'Yeah, there's a prison there as well.' He knew his way around England by the location of prisons and former cell mates.

Anyway, he soon fucked off, and then so did we. It wasn't exactly comfortable in the bunk bed, but I was knackered and soon dozed off. I kept waking up though, thinking I was on North Sea Ferries with the way the train was rocking. But we were on our way to Paris for a few days relaxation, and I managed a few hours' sleep.

Day 11, Tuesday 23 June

I was woken up at about 6.30 a.m. by the conductor announcing that we'd be arriving in Paris in half an hour. It was all in French, but me being a clever git understood most of what he said. I opened the door of our cabin and was nearly blinded by the daylight, and then went off for a tab at the end of the carriage, gazing out the window at the French countryside flying past. Didn't think much of the tab though, so I chucked it in the bog and had a piss.

So half an hour later we arrived at the Gare d'Austerlitz in Paris, and feeling weary eyed we got off the train. We got the usual welcome – several dozen riot police along the platform and also outside the station. What a fucking piss take! Did they really expect a hundred or so English to riot at a train station at 7 a.m.? It's no wonder we came to resent the way that we were treated by the French authorities.

Anyway, the three of us left the station and went for a walk, and ended up sitting next to the River Seine for about 15 minutes, trying to wake up and decide what to do. We went to McDonalds for breakfast, two egg Macmuffins, orange juice and black coffee, and then back to the station and asked a bloke on the information stall about local accommodation. He wasn't really helpful and just gave us the address of the main tourist office in the Champs-Élysées, which was miles away.

So we walked up the road and asked a copper if there were many hotels nearby. He pointed up the road, and I couldn't help noticing how shocked he was that *un hooligan anglais* spoke reasonably fluent French. Anyway, we walked up the road and managed to find a fairly decent hotel, just over five minutes' walk away from the station.

We were quite surprised that they weren't full, but this was Paris and we were just glad to find accommodation at our first attempt, so we checked in and paid for the room. Our room was quite good, three beds, a shower and a bog, and we all crashed out for a bit, still feeling knackered after not much sleep on the train. I heard the cleaner just outside the room, and I went out to ask her if she knew where I could wash my clothes. She didn't speak a word of English and had a funny French dialect, but she said that she would do it. Sorted! So we all gave her our smelly, dirty washing and two hours later she brought it back, washed, dried and ironed! Couldn't believe it. We felt a bit guilty though because we never gave her any money, but what the fuck, she never asked.

So after that we left the hotel and headed off to the Stade de France, where we'd try and get tickets for the Italy v Austria game. We walked down to the station and got the Metro up to St Denis. I was wearing my England hat that I'd bought in Toulouse, and was wandering what sort of reaction I'd get from the Italians. Mel had his England Three Lions' sun hat on, but it was a bit more subtle than the St George's flag and England on the front of my hat. Never had a hint of trouble though.

The Stade de France looked very impressive as we walked up to it. Now we'd have the task of finding tickets. After walking around for a bit we started asking for tickets, but were quoted stupid prices again, £150–£200. We weren't going to pay more than £50–£60 for a match we weren't bothered about. We just wanted to see another World Cup match, especially in the Stade de France.

We managed to get two tickets for £50 each, and then about half an hour later, we got one for £80; we just split the difference and paid £60 each. So after another walk around the stadium, we went in to take up our seats, with plenty of time before kick off. Me and Mel had the two seats in the neutral section, and Matt had a ticket in the Italian section. I noticed that there were very few police around compared to England matches, even for a stadium as big as the Stade de France.

It was a great sight walking out into the Stade de France, and I have to say it's better than Wembley. We'll just have to see what they can do when they redevelop Wembley over the next few years – can't be outdone by the French. Anyway, after finding our seats, me and Mel went to find a place for his Darlo flag, the one of Toulouse fame, and put it on a barrier in front of some empty seating. The stadium soon filled up, and although there were quite a few Austrians, there were slightly more Italians in the ground.

The Wops just sang that shitty, irritating chant, 'I-Tal-Ia, I-Tal-Ia', which is nearly as irritating as that monotonous crap sung by Rochdale fans, 'Da-ale, Da-ale'! But although the Austrians had several boring renditions of 'Ostereich, Ostereich', they kept on singing 'Stand up if You Hate Germans', and of course they all did stand up. It was well funny.

As we were sat there, we noticed some Eyetie was complaining to a steward about our flag. Cheeky twat! But then, ten minutes later, the dirty little fucking Wops had untied the flag at one end, and half of it was hanging down. So me and Mel went up there to sort it out. Mel tied it back up, and some Wop said something, but when Mel replied they said they didn't speak English. Then some greasy as fuck Wop with a Pizza box pattern (or is it the Italian flag?) painted on his face, said to me, 'Hey, why this?' pointing at Darlington on the flag. I said, '' cos it's my team, that's who I support.' But he then said, 'No. Why ... here. Why here?' pointing around the stadium. So I replied, 'cos it's the World Cup, and I'm here. Look, there's Sweden and Mexico flags here as well.' Then I just stared the cunt in the eye, leaned forward slightly, and said, 'It's not a problem is it?' He just sat there, sunk right back into his seat, and didn't say a word. He shit himself, which is just as well, 'cos any more shit from that greasy fucking Wop bastard and I would have chinned the cunt. He must have thought, *Oh mama mia, hooligan Inglesi*. Soft bastard! He was just jealous because I won the lottery of life and was born English, whereas he came 87th and was born a Wop.

Anyway, after that they never touched the flag. Looked like I'd done the job. So we sat back and waited for the match to start, and watched the video of the Carnival de Paris on the giant screen, which produced a cheer from the two of us when the kids painted in the flag of St George scored against the kids painted in Italian flags. And then the teams came out for the match. When they were all lined up and the Italian national anthem played, I couldn't help thinking that it sounded just like an ice-cream van – 'Der der der-der, der der der-der', so I said to Mel, 'Sounds like the ice-cream van's here.'

When the match started, Italy looked as though they'd win it easily, but Austria played better after a while. We wanted Austria to win, especially as Italy would have gone out if they'd lost and Chile won in the other game. Plus the fact Darlo's 'Super' Mario Dorner is Austrian. But Italy soon went 1–0 up, and late on in the game it was 2–0, but just as we'd taken the flag down, Austria got a penalty and made it 2–1. It was too late though, and it finished 2–1, so Austria went out and Italy went through. Not a bad game though. Despite all their cheating and diving, we had to show our appreciation for some of the good football that the Italians had played. Well, we clapped our hands about three or four times, didn't want to overdo it.

Although the Stade de France is very good, I'd noticed on the TV that there was never much atmosphere there, and that was the case for the game we'd just seen. I think the number of press and corporate ticket holders probably had something to do with it, but even when France were there the atmosphere was never that good. But that's the French. I think the big gap between the top of the stadium and the roof probably had something to do with it, but that alone wouldn't have that much effect. I couldn't help thinking how great the atmosphere would be if England were there though. We'd take over the stadium, just like we'd done in Marseilles and Toulouse. Well, the final was to be played there.

Anyway, after leaving the stadium we got to where we'd arranged to meet Matt and waited around for him. As we were stood around I noticed that the back of my neck was sunburnt, and it hurt like fuck whenever the slightest bit of sun shone on it. I didn't bother putting sun cream on there because I'd been in France for a week or so, and didn't expect to get burnt anywhere else, although I was wearing a low necked t-shirt.

A load of wankers from London, but obviously of Italian origin as they were wearing Italy shirts, walked past singing 'There's only one Bobby Baggio'. Tossers! We noticed Neville Southall walk past down below us, the former Everton goalkeeper, before Matt finally turned up half an hour later. He said there were massive queues of people where he'd come out, and it'd taken ages to get round. He said he'd enjoyed the game and was sat right near the top of the stadium, and could even see the Eiffel Tower from where he was, as well as the Darlo flag.

So we headed off towards the Metro station, and on the way someone who was about seven feet tall stopped Mel and pointed at the small Darlo badge pinned to his England hat, and said, 'What's this, who is it?' Mel said it's Darlington, a team from the north east of England, and the bloke said, 'I'm Russian, I'm collecting tickets, perhaps you can give me ticket,' in a spooky as fuck Russian accent. We told him no, because we wanted them for souvenirs, and noticed he had a wad of about 50 used tickets from the match, which he'd presumably got from stopping every other person. Weird fucker!

We soon got down to the Metro station, and after a short wait we were on our way back to the Gare d'Austerlitz. We decided to get something to eat and drink at the café next to our hotel, and then watch the final games from Group A on the TV – Norway v Brazil and Scotland v Morocco. With a bit of luck, Norway would beat Brazil and the Jocks would be out in the first round yet again. So we arrived back at the Gare d'Austerlitz and walked up to the café. We sat down but then the waiter moved us to another table. We already thought he was a twat! We all decided to have roast chicken and chips, with a beer, but after taking our orders he comes back and says the chicken's off. He then stood there expecting us to make an instant decision about an alternative, when the only choice was 20 different salads or horse burger. I'm so hungry I could eat a horse, I thought. Not that fucking hungry though. So we just ended up choosing salad. But when the waiter took our orders, he literally walked straight out of the café and across the fucking road, lighting up a tab on the way. He just disappeared. Cheeky fucker. Fuck that, we thought, and decided to fuck off and try somewhere else. If the waiter can just fuck off like that, so can we. Tosser!

So we got up and left the café, and went down the road and found a much better place, although it was totally empty. We sat down, and the waiter was straight over to take our orders, drinks arrived within two minutes and food within five minutes (obviously microwaved). I had a big jug of white wine and drunk it like I'd drink a pint. The food was all right, and although I could have drunk another jug of wine, we went back to the hotel because we were all a bit knackered, laughing at the waiter at the other café on the way.

Back in the room and we just crashed out watching the football. Norway v Brazil was on TV, but they kept showing the score from the Scotland game. Funny as fuck – they got beat 3–0 by Morocco, with Jim Leighton in goal making himself look like a clown. It would get better though. Brazil took the lead with less than a quarter of an hour left, and upon hearing this the Moroccans went mad celebrating, knowing that Norway had to win to stop Morocco going through to the next round. But Norway scored with just over five minutes left, and then got a dodgy penalty which I was happy to see go in, and that was it. Scotland and Morocco out. Ha ha! What was Scotland's World Cup song? 'Don't come home too soon'? First Round again. So after that bit of entertainment, it was time to crash out, ahead of a day's sightseeing in Paris. I had to chuck off two thick blankets from the bed first though, because it was boiling. Didn't they realise that it was summer, and hot as fuck? Anyway, soon got to sleep.

Day 12, Wednesday 24 June

This was to be a day of seeing the sights of Paris, so once we were all up we set off for the Metro station, stopping for breakfast on the way. I'd decided to wear my newly washed England shirt, as well as the hat, just so everyone knew we're English and proud of it. Me and Mel both took our flags with us, the plan being to get them out at the top of the Eiffel Tower. So after asking directions from some gorgeous French girls who worked at the station's World Cup information office, the three of us got the Metro to near the Eiffel Tower, and walked over to the tower itself, which is fucking massive.

On the way there were a load of artists trying to make money out of tourists, drawing those crap pictures of people's faces that are supposed to be funny. One of them persuaded me to sit down so he could draw me, after saying I didn't have to buy it, and that he was drawing it for himself. So I sat there while he waffled on and drew a picture of my face. When he showed me it I just laughed – it was a total bag of shite. Looked nothing like me. He wanted 100 francs for it but there was no way I was paying that (or anything) for something I didn't want. He went down to 30 francs but I still said no and he was gutted. But I did tell him before he started. Mel and Matt both got pictures drawn by two others, Matt did the same as me but Mel bought his for 20 francs. Another English bloke asked me how much they were charging, and I said, '£10 and the pictures are shite', after which he thanked me.

So after that we headed off to the Eiffel Tower, stopping at the 'football village' on the way, which was just a few five-a-side pitches, shooting contest (with footballs, not guns), and some tents full of crappy souvenirs. We got to the Eiffel Tower and joined one of the queues for the lift to the top floor. I'd been there before ten years earlier but had only gone to the first floor, and the other two hadn't been there before, so we were quite looking forward to it. After a twenty-minute wait we bought our tickets and went to the lift, which took us up to the second floor, where we had to change lifts. So yet again we were in another queue, but after a while we got into the lift up to the top. As we were going up I was reminded of the scene on 'FIFA 98' for the Playstation, where they show the view from the lift whenever you chose to play the game at Paris. Which is nice.

And then we were there. The top of the Eiffel Tower. We were inside the enclosed bit to start with, which has photos and pointers to the landmarks of Paris, as well as directions to places all around the world. Couldn't see one for Darlington or Osmotherley. We went up the steps to the outside part, which was packed as fuck. An Italian got out his crappy flag and held it up for a photo, but it was only about two feet long. So around the corner we went, where there were fewer people, and admired the view of Paris. It's a decent view from up there, and we could see the Stade de France, Parc des Princes, the Louvre, Notre Dame, Arc de Triomphe, Sacré Coeur, and an infinite number of other buildings. Then it was photo time, so first I got out my St George's flag with Darlington FC on it, held it up and

Day 12, Wednesday 24 June

Mel took a picture. What a sight – flag, England shirt, hat – 'we're Darlo, we took your Eiffel Tower', were the most appropriate words. A QPR fan came around the corner and said, 'He's got his old Darlington flag out,' so after I took a photo of Mel with his flag, which wasn't easy given the size of it, we stood and talked to the QPR fans for a while. It was them who first told us about the booze ban in Lens for the Colombia game.

We stood there admiring the view for a bit longer, and saw the Louvre museum. It didn't look all that far away when looking from the top of the Eiffel Tower, so we decided that we'd walk to it. We headed down for the lift, and after short wait were on our way back down. We got to the second floor and stopped off at the bar for a quick drink. I was in need of refuelling so I had a beer. After that we waited around for the lift down to the bottom. Some irritating as fuck French tour guide was waffling on and on to these upper class Americans, who were trying to act posh, which did my head in a bit, given the size of the queue. When we finally got on to the lift, Mel and Matt had spotted Paul Durkin there, England's World Cup referee, who had been in charge of the Italy v Austria match. We got talking to him and he said he didn't think that he'd get another game in the World Cup, after making a few mistakes the day before. He fell for a few of the cheating Eyetie's dives and play acting, but after a while I thought he'd done okay.

Anyway, we got down to the bottom of the Eiffel Tower, got someone to take a picture of us with Paul Durkin, and then we set off towards the Louvre museum. It was yet another boiling hot day, and we tried our best to walk along in the shade of the trees. Like I said, the distance to the Louvre didn't look that far from the top of the Eiffel Tower, but it fucking was. We crossed over the River Seine and kept walking towards the Louvre, but didn't seem to be getting much nearer. We wanted to stop for a beer, but for some strange reason there were no bars around at all. We passed the entrance to the tunnel where Princess Diana was killed in August 1997, and the statue there had been turned into some sort of shrine, with pictures, flowers, letters and graffiti from all over the world. Quite sad, but we didn't bother taking a photo or anything.

We headed off again, and walked past the Champs-Élysées, still unable to find a decent-looking bar. We asked some women what direction the Louvre was in, and in reply to Matt asking if they spoke English, one said, 'Yes, sir!' Americans! Why are Yanks always so much over the top? Anyway, they pointed us in the right direction, and we could finally see the place. After walking along a row of expensive-looking shops where I got a bottle of water, we walked into the grounds of the Louvre. My feet were getting pretty fucked after eleven days of wearing the same boots for most of the time, and walking miles every day in hot weather. But I kept going and we finally arrived at the entrance, after trying unsuccessfully to find a side entrance where we could sneak in.

I'd been to the Louvre in 1988, when I was over with the school, so I wasn't too bothered about going. But we were there, the other two hadn't been before, and a bit of culture would make a change. The entrance is through a glass pyramid, where you go down the escalator and into the main hall to buy your ticket. It was as hot as fuck in there. The stupid bastards build glass pyramids, which are effectively like greenhouses in summer, and don't bother with any air conditioning or fans in the place.

Day 12, Wednesday 24 June

So anyway, we bought our tickets and then spent the next two hours walking around the museum, which is fucking massive, looking at Egyptian artefacts, loads of paintings including the Mona Lisa, sculptures and other stuff. My feet were fucked at the end of it, and I was gagging for a pint. It was still hot outside when we got out, even though it was getting on for 7 p.m. We decided to get on a bus using our Paris transport day passes, and get off wherever looked decent enough, for something to eat and a few beers.

I haven't a clue where we got off the bus, but it was central Paris, a couple of miles north of the Eiffel Tower, and there were a few decent looking cafés around. We found a café and the waiter took us to a table, and brought us an English menu. It was a decent place, on the corner of a road, and there were a mixture of tourists and locals there. First thing was first – booze! Me and Matt both ordered a litre of beer each, while Mel was on the red wine again. He was determined to try a bit of French cuisine while we were over there, so he ordered snails for a starter. Uurghh! I'd had them years ago and didn't think much of them, so I didn't bother trying any of Mel's, like Matt did.

The main course was gorgeous (just like the waitress) – roast chicken and chips – and had to be washed down with another beer. It was probably one of the best meals we'd had in France, and was just what we needed after walking several miles in the heat, seeing the sights of Paris. The food was good, the beer was good, and the service was good, so we even left a 60 franc tip.

After leaving the café we got the Metro back over to the Gare d'Austerlitz. The Paris Metro is hard as fuck to work out, nothing like the good old London Underground. For a

81

start, they've got two systems running together, the Metro and RER, which is basically the same but often runs overground, and the trains are bigger. The worst thing was the shitty maps they had in the stations. One type was some kind of surreal crap that didn't really tell you anything, and the actual Metro map showed all of the lines in very similar colours to each other. Not like London, where there's red, blue, green, black, brown, etc, with a nice clear key to the map. No, these dumb bastards have the lines in yellow, orange, greeney-yellow, orangey-red, and any other pus colour you can think of. And they label the lines at the end of each one, instead of having a simple colour key.

Another thing about the Paris Metro is the amount of beggars on the trains. One day some Asian women got on to the train, carrying a baby, tits out for all to see, and started whaling some shite like, '*s'il vous plaît, donnez moi l'argent, s'il vous plaît*', in the most irritating fucking voice you can imagine. Everyone just ignored the bitch. Another time some smelly bastard got on, but he was some sort of weirdo intellectual, going on about all sorts of crap, but still asking for money. I thought Mel was going to chin him the way he was staring at the scrounging bastard, but he was just trying not to laugh at him.

But, despite all of that, we managed to find our way around, and got back to the hotel, stopping off for a few cans of beer on the way. When we got there, we put our feet up and watched Eurosport. This time it was Spain's turn to go out in the First Round, which was funny considering they were one of the pre-tournament favourites. So another day in Paris over with, and a good one at that, Darlo having taken the Eiffel Tower, after taking the Stade de France on the previous day. One more day in Paris left, and we planned to go and watch Belgium v South Korea at the Parc des Princes.

Day 13, Thursday 25 June

Our last full day in Paris started as usual, getting up mid-morning and me getting a drink from the vending machine downstairs. While I was down there I asked reception if they had a needle and cotton – one of the strips on the corner of the flag had come off when we were at the campsite in Fréjus. I knew I was crap at sewing. The bloke on reception asked what it was for, and when I said my flag, he said, 'Denmark?' to which I replied, '*non, Angleterre.*' So of course they came out with the usual shite, 'Hooligan? Ha, ha, ha.' Twat! He must be thick as fuck if he didn't know I was English. We'd spent the two previous days there, walking in speaking English, I'd been wearing my England hat all of the time, and my England shirt on the previous day. And he thought I was Danish! Thick fucker!

Anyway, they gave me a needle and cotton, and I went back upstairs to sort out the flag, which didn't take too long. And then we were ready, so the three of us set of to the Parc des Princes for Belgium v South Korea, taking both of the flags and me and Mel both wearing our England hats. We stopped for a sandwich on the way to the Metro station, and then got the Metro over to the Porte de St Cloud station, near the Parc des Princes.

We weren't too bothered about the match, and weren't going to pay more than about 300 francs for a ticket. But we were there for football, and it would be another World Cup match to see, and another World Cup venue to visit. We decided to wait until nearer kick-off time before buying a ticket, because that's when it would be cheaper, especially as it was hardly a big match, unless you're unlucky enough to be Belgian.

When we got out of the Metro station, there were loads of Belgians about, some in daft fancy dress and a few just looked like nutters. But fuck it, we're English, they wouldn't have a go at us. After going to a cash machine and a tobacconist, we went up nearer to the stadium and walked around. People were already selling tickets, but for shit prices. Some twat was asking 1,500 francs, and when we said 300 francs, he said, 'No, I think you're joking.' 'You're the one that's joking mate,' was the immediate response. Cheeky fucker. As if some English lads would pay £150 to watch Belgium v South Korea!

Ten minutes later, after a bit more of a walk around the stadium, some nice looking lass was selling tickets. We offered her 200 francs each, and after consulting her friend she agreed, so we gave her the money and were sorted. Three tickets together for £20 each. I know that I've already had a go at the government's crappy advert about World Cup tickets ('all tickets have the purchaser's name on'), but this one really took the piss. Our tickets had the French girl's name on, Mademoiselle something, which was no problem whatsoever. So up yours Jack Straw.

So after getting our match tickets sorted, it was time for some beer. We walked down the road away from the stadium and found a small bar that was mainly full of Belgians. We got the beers in and sat at a table outside, watching the world go by. Some Huddersfield lads (there were about eight or nine of them) came over and sat with us, and we had a good chat about Darlo, Huddersfield, Arsenal, the World Cup, Paris, and whatever else. They were sound as fuck, and we arranged to meet them back at that bar after the match. That's two tournaments running now that I've ended up with Huddersfield fans who've been sound, having met a couple after England v Scotland in Euro 96. So with kick off approaching, it was time to head off to the match, so we left the Huddersfield fans and went to the stadium.

When we got there it was the usual checks, with no attention being paid to the name on the ticket, and then we went in to find our seats. We were behind one of the goals, just along from the section containing the South Korea fans. As the national anthems were being played, me and Mel went down to the front to put our Darlo flags up, seeing as everyone was stood up anyway. There were no barriers to tie them to, so we just draped them over the wall at the front, and then went back up to our seats.

The Parc des Princes is not a bad stadium, though obviously not as good as the Stade de France. Most of the people were a combination of Belgians and French, with a few thousand South Koreans, plus the usual amount of non-French neutrals such as ourselves. I'd noticed that virtually every match in the World Cup had England or Scotland flags in view. The weird thing about the Belgians was that they kept singing in English – 'We love you Belgium, we do...'

Once the match started it seemed as though Belgium would walk all over South Korea, especially when they scored early on. Belgium had to win that game and hope that Mexico lost to Holland, because they were a couple of points behind them in third place. By half-time they were looking safe, even though it was still only 1–0, because Mexico were losing to Holland.

In the second half South Korea started playing really well, and the Belgians started to panic a bit. The Korean fans were making loads of noise, banging their drums, chanting and waving their arms in unison. The World Cup tends to lose some of its colour once the likes of South Korea go out. But their fans were soon rewarded when they scored the equaliser midway through the second half. The fans went mad, and most neutrals celebrated the goals, leaving the Belgians stunned. They were going out, which was funny. The South Koreans nearly scored again, before Belgium put them under loads of pressure, but to no avail. So it ended 1–1, and Belgium were out of the World Cup, finishing two points behind second-placed Mexico who'd drawn with Holland.

Some of the South Korean women were gorgeous, so maybe having the 2002 World Cup in Japan and South Korea isn't such a bad idea after all. The Koreans were celebrating their good result, and the Belgians left the stadium, on their way home. They didn't look all that gutted though, considering they'd just been knocked out of the World Cup. If that was England we'd be going mad. I was just hoping that we'd do the business against Colombia, where we had to avoid defeat to go through.

So after leaving what turned to be our last World Cup match we'd go to, we went back to the bar that we'd been in earlier with the Huddersfield fans. There were quite a few Belgians there at that point, and a few Koreans as well. We got the beers in and then the Huddersfield lads turned up, so we sat talking to them for ages. It was weird how the bar virtually emptied within ten minutes, just because of a dozen English being there. Mind you, I don't think anyone would have argued with us.

The Huddersfield lot had decided to find the Sacré Coeur, because there was meant to be a load of good bars there, so we decided to go with them for a piss up, feeling good after several post-match beers. So the twelve of us went down to the Metro station, where we got on a train once someone worked out where to go. It was funny on that train, a dozen English lads spread out along one end of the carriage, which was fairly full of locals. We did the usual thing and made sure that everyone knew we were English, whistling 'The Great Escape' theme tune and singing 'Vindaloo' among other things. We weren't being out of order or anything, but the French didn't know what to make of us, probably thinking, *c'est les hooligans anglais.* We're England, we took your Metro!

When we got to the place we were going to, we left the station, walked down the road and realised that we'd got off one stop too soon. We went to the nearest bar anyway, and ordered the beers. I dunno what beer I had, but it was fucking disgusting. It was kind of like beer's equivalent of Earl Grey tea. So I ordered a different beer next time, which wasn't much better. But it turned out to be third time lucky when I just fucked off the draught beer and got a bottle. Someone asked the staff where the Sacré Coeur was, and they were told it was a couple of miles away.

So we all sat down for a bit drinking beer. Four of the Huddersfield lot were determined to find this place, so they set off, leaving the rest of us behind. We weren't too bothered about walking a few miles to try and find somewhere that probably wasn't that good anyway. So me,

Matt, Mel and the remaining Huddersfield fans went off in search of something to eat nearby.

They wanted something crap like a McDonalds, but we'd got sick of that place and wanted something better. As we walked down the street we found an Indian restaurant. After spending the previous two weeks singing 'Vindaloo', we just had to go for a curry. The others still wanted their burgers or whatever, so we left them and went into the curry house.

When we got in there, we were greeted by a really cheerful Indian waiter, who must have been the manager. He kept clapping his hands and grinning, and I got the impression that he was the first restaurant owner in France who was actually pleased to have some English customers. He took us to a table downstairs and took our drink orders. A few minutes later the waitress came with three pints of Carlsberg. It seems that every single Indian restaurant in the world has Carlsberg. It was nice though, and so was the waitress. She kept telling us that she was from Nepal, and smiled nearly as much as the manager. She was no stunner, but I would have given her one.

Anyway, enough of my obsession with waitresses. We ordered poppadams for starters, and then me and Mel ordered Chicken Vindaloo, which just had to be done given the occasion. Matt bottled it and had a Chicken Korma, but as he pointed out, he wouldn't be suffering in the morning.

It was good in that place, with some sort of eastern music playing, and various ornaments and decorations around the walls. Seemed a bit more classy than your average Indian in England, which all seem to have red walls and a slightly tacky appearance. We kept talking about travelling to India and Nepal, but that was probably the beer talking.

I wouldn't mind going over there, but I think the heat and the insects would totally do my head in.

Anyway, after the poppadams and more beer the curries arrived. The chicken was still on the bone which was strange for a curry. The Vindaloo was hot as fuck, which Matt found quite amusing, but despite a red face, runny nose, sweaty forehead and my mouth on fire, I really enjoyed the Vindaloo. Fucking lovely it was. Once I'd finished I was in need of more beer to cool my mouth down, and after a chat with the staff we headed off back to the Metro station. The service in the restaurant was the best we'd had so far, and the food was nice, so we left a decent tip.

When we got to the station there weren't many people about, so we couldn't resist several renditions of 'Vindaloo', seeing as we'd just eaten one. It sounded quite good in the Metro station, 'Vindaloo, Vindaloo, Vindaloo Vindaloo na-na … and we all like Vindaloo … we're gonna score one more than you … England!' Sound as fuck. We ended up singing that most of the way back to the hotel, stopping off at a pub and then the shop nearby to get some more drinks.

Once we were back in the hotel room, it was decided that we needed to hear my World Cup special tape again, which we hadn't listened to since the train to Toulouse. So on it went, and I opened up the windows which overlooked a busy junction, and stood there dancing around with my flag, singing along to the tape loud as fuck for all to hear. The other two were dancing around the room, singing away, and then took turns with the flag by the window. It was a great laugh, singing 'Vindaloo' yet again, as well as 'Three Lions' ('It's coming home, it's coming home, it's coming, football's coming home'), 'This Time', 'The Great Escape', 'Rule

Britannia' and all the rest. Eventually we were all feeling fucked and crashed out, having had a good end to our last day in Paris.

Day 14, Friday 26 June

It was finally time to leave Paris to go up to Lens for England's final group game against Colombia. We didn't have tickets, and knew we'd have to pay at least £300 for them, but we thought we'd go up there anyway, have a look around the town and watch the match in a bar somewhere. But to start the day off I was suffering from the Vindaloo. Big style! First shit at 6.30 a.m. Not too bad. The next one at 9 a.m. woke the other two up. The pre-shit fart echoed around the toilet bowl, then came a runny shit, then I burped and then blew my nose. What a fucking noise. I knew the other two had woken up when I heard Matt say 'faacking 'ell'. But then after a couple more craps I was ready to leave, suffering from a slight 'ring of fire'.

So we left the hotel for the last time, walked down to the Gare d'Austerlitz, got the Metro up to the Gare du Nord, and got a TGV train to Lille, where we'd been 12 days earlier to go to Marseilles. We never had time to buy the reservation ticket, so we had to get it on the train, which cost us three times as much. It's fucking stupid, having to buy reservation tickets for the TGV train, so we had to pay 60 francs extra just to sit in one of those poxy pull-down seats in the corridor. Why it costs 40 francs more to buy the reservation on the train than buying it in the station is anyone's guess.

Day 14, Friday 26 June

Anyway, the journey to Lille was fairly uneventful, other than a couple of ticket touts sat near us whose mobile phones never stopped ringing. Once we got to Lille we tried dumping our rucksacks at the station, but someone said the lockers were unavailable. Bollocks! We had planned to dump our bags at the station and get the last train to Amsterdam after the match, so after finding out train times to Lens we ended up walking around looking for a hotel for the night, seeing as we couldn't leave our bags at the station. It was the same old story though, everywhere was full.

But then we had the idea of trying the Lille Europe station, which was only a quarter of a mile away. Once there, we were able to leave our bags in a left luggage place, the only drawback being that it shut at about 10 p.m. and didn't open until 6.30 a.m., so we would have to doss at the train station. At least we'd got rid of our bags anyway, so we headed back over to the other train station to wait for the train to Lens.

There were loads of English about, and you could tell apart those such as ourselves who'd been over in France for two weeks, and those that had just arrived that day, doing it the cheap way and only going for a day trip, seeing as Lens is only about 50 miles away from Calais. With all those extra English around, we knew we'd have no chance of a ticket, because demand would be that great that the ticket prices would be a complete piss take.

So after waiting around for a while, the train finally arrived to take us to Lens. It was one of those double-decker trains that you sometimes see on the Continent, and was packed full of English, seeing as it was a World Cup special train. We sat there on the way to Lens, expecting to face a shit load of police, after the Germans had gone on the rampage there five days earlier and put a copper in a coma. Plus the fact all the papers had been full of stories about the famous English hooligans.

When we got to Lens, there weren't all that many pigs at the station, but there was plenty of press there, including an open top double-decker bus from *The Sun* newspaper. The cheeky bastards were giving out plastic England bowler hats with *The Sun* written on them, after all that they'd said about us during the previous two weeks (or should that be previous 30 years?). 'A disgrace to our country' they called us, and now they were giving out shitty plastic hats. I can't believe some people were actually taking the hats as well, instead of doing the bus over and kicking the fuck out of the tabloid scum. Still, that would only have given them more shit to write about us, and given the riot police something to do earlier than expected.

We left the station and went for a walk around the town centre. There were loads of English around, and we'd literally invaded Lens, which only has a population of about 35,000 people. Within ten minutes we'd already decided that Lens was a shit town. We'd heard rumours about a booze ban, and after walking around and finding nearly everywhere closed, as well as being sold alcohol-free piss-water beer in a shit café, the rumours were proved to be true.

We only wanted to drink beer, get pissed, have a laugh, and watch the match. But no, the shitty French authorities denied us that right, as if we're fucking sub-human or something. We noticed a large crowd of English at the side of the road, flags up on the fence behind, singing, 'If it wasn't for the English you'd be Krauts' at a load of press and a few coppers across the road. It's gonna go off there later on, was the conclusion as we walked past. Might have to join them then, was the response. We carried on our desperate search for beer, which was made worse by the sight of loads of people carrying bags full of duty-free beer that they'd bought on the way over to France earlier that day. As we walked down the road we noticed an old couple looking out of their open window, and the bloke had the biggest fucking nose I've ever seen. It must have been plasticine or something. It put the Yid in Toulouse to shame anyway. Fucking unreal it was. Just a humongous blob stuck in the middle of his face. Which made us all laugh like fuck.

After trying a garage (they usually sell alcohol in France), which had the beer covered over with black plastic sacks, we decided to go and join the crowd back down the road. We got there and stood at the side of the road, just down from the main group of people who were singing at the press and pigs, as well as chucking a bit of beer around. I asked some West Bromwich fans if they had any beer for sale, but they just gave us all one for nothing. Sound as fuck. I drunk the bottle of beer in about two minutes, and could have done with another twenty.

But then the riot police moved in and mobbed up down the road, about 40 yards away from us. 'It's gonna go off in a minute,' said one of the West Brom fans. 'Better get ready to move lads, it's gonna go off.' We couldn't really see what was happening, but knew the pigs were gonna have a go, just because a few lads were blocking the road and chucking a bit of beer around. People were slowly starting to move down the road, and then that was it. Sshhhiiiiitt! Everyone was suddenly legging it down the road, as the riot police did a full on baton charge at us. Even though instinct told me not to run, when everyone around you is running away from a mob of riot police with helmets, shields and batons who are charging towards you, it's best to follow. It was sheer fucking panic, as we were chased through the tunnel under the railway, with people in full flight chucking beer bottles over their heads, which were smashing all around me. I took my hat off thinking it'd fall off, and then became convinced that a bottle would hit me on the head, or I'd fall over a bottle and get batted by the pigs, or I'd get a baton over my head any second. It felt like they were right behind me, but when everyone stopped running and turned around, the pig scum had stopped at the other end of the tunnel, and proceeded to form a line which effectively closed the road off.

My feet were fucked enough from all the miles of walking during two hot weeks in France, wearing the same boots for most of the time, but that bit of running had burst a blister on the bottom of my foot, right in the middle, and it hurt like fuck. Once we realised that the police weren't coming down to where we were, we sat on the roundabout for a while, and watched any developments up the road.

A few lads were trying to get a mob together to steam the pigs, but when there's several bus loads of riot police facing you, with full riot gear protecting them, it doesn't really inspire you to have a go at the cunts, no matter how pissed off you feel. So we just sat there for a while, talking to some Chelsea fans, and then came to the conclusion that the police would wait until just before kick off, block off the area that we were in, and nick everyone without a match ticket. It was time to fuck off out of there, so we went down a road that shouldn't have been more than ten minutes' walk to the station. I asked a copper which way it was to the station, knowing that there would be no chance of going the way we came. The twat said it was about five kilometres away, and I thought he was taking the piss. I asked why the other road was closed and he just replied, 'Hooligans.' Fucking twat. I argued with him for a bit (in French), but didn't really have a go at the cunt because he had a load of kids with him.

So we went further down the road in search of the station, following a group of other English down some side street. We walked for ages down past this industrial estate, which like the rest of the town was closed because of *les hooligans anglais*, not that I wanted any bricks or metal or anything from there. There was about 20 of us walking down the road, trying to get to the train station so we could get out of that shit fucking town. It was like *The Great Escape* (from Lens), so I started whistling the theme tune from the film, and everyone joined in, which was followed by 'Colonel Bogey'. What a moment! We must have looked a real sight. Twenty English lads, pissed off, being followed by a police helicopter overhead, whistling war themes.

As we got further down the road, there were some people going the other way, saying that there was no way to the station down there, just a motorway and about ten railway lines. We had a look anyway, and a couple of lads were walking up the hard shoulder of the motorway. How long before they get nicked? As we stood around thinking about what to do, some train security guards and police came over with dogs, making sure we never jumped the fence and ran across the lines. I asked them if there was another way to the station, which was literally 200 yards across the railway lines, but they just took the piss and said to keep walking. Wankers!

We headed off back the way we came, and by this stage

I was getting really pissed off. We were soon back at the roundabout where we were earlier, and decided to have a go at getting through under the bridge, where we'd been chased through earlier. We told the pig bastard that we wanted to get to the train station, so we could leave that shit town, but they'd obviously been told not to let anyone through unless they had a match ticket, and the cunts just ignored us after a while. So we were trapped.

What a complete fuck up. The French tourism minister says, 'Come to France, with or without tickets, enjoy the World Cup atmosphere.' So what do they do? They close the whole fucking town, no beer anywhere, just because we're English. Pure fucking discrimination. If there's one nation in the world you can be racist against it's the English. Treated like shit wherever we go. I now know what the blacks in the southern United States must have felt like in the 1950s. Well, not quite.

But the French authorities in Lens just didn't have a clue. What did they expect when they closed all the bars down? Thirty thousand English to walk around admiring the architecture? It's only natural that we'd group up and have a sing-song, and drink any available beer, but the miserable French cunts didn't understand that. We just wanted a laugh and watch the match, either in the stadium or in a bar. Even in Toulouse it wasn't too bad. Okay, they closed the bars three hours early and cancelled the annual festival because of us, but the police kept a low profile and there was virtually no trouble, certainly not with locals. And there was certainly no trouble with Romanians in Toulouse or the Colombians in Lens, so the action of the authorities was totally unjustified.

And what a fuck up of a town Lens is. Where the riot

police chased us to we could only get to the train station by taking a four- or five-mile detour, seeing as they'd closed the main road off to non-ticket holders. Why don't they build a fucking bridge over the railway lines just down the road? It would have saved a lot of unnecessary aggravation. Stupid French bastards!

Anyway, after trying the bridge, we asked another traffic copper how we could get to the station. He told us to walk one kilometre down the road and turn left at the first round-about, and it was about four kilometres after that. So, with fuck all else to do and less than three hours until kick off, we decided to give it a go. I was well pissed off, and was tempted to do some damage to that shit town. But what was the point? The locals had done fuck all, and the traders were probably pissed off at all the trade they were losing. But the way we felt, we kept saying, 'That French copper that the Germans put in a coma – I hope he fucking dies!'

So after walking for 15 minutes down the road, we got to a roundabout, started turning left, and realised it was a motorway down there, but we thought what the fuck and kept going. Until a police van pulls up ten seconds later, some black copper gets out and says, 'You can't go that way, it's a highway,' which he repeated about ten times, especially when we said some other copper told us to go that way, and we only wanted to get to the train station to get out of the shit town. But it was no use arguing, and we ended up walking back. I could have killed someone, but thought a very loud shout of 'Bollocks' would be better in the long-term. It certainly turned a few heads anyway.

We got back to the roundabout yet again, and decided to give the bridge another ago. Same old story, shitty fucking riot police not letting us past, even when I said (in French) that we just wanted to get to the station and leave the town. The cunts just ignored us, and then when a couple of Cockneys tried getting through, one copper broke out from the line and pushed him, raised his baton and said, 'Go that way.' So there were five of us there, and the Cockneys started shouting at the coppers, which we joined in with – 'Take that helmet off, drop your shield and your baton and come round the corner, then we'll see how fucking hard you are.' The Cockney summed it all up there. Fucking pigs would be soft as shite without their riot gear. But rather than hang around and get nicked we fucked off down the road, as did the two Cockneys. We had a go at a foreign camera crew who were stood around looking to film trouble. I said, 'I bet you're not fucking filming this, it's a fucking disgrace,' and various things were added by the others. They wanted fuck all to do with it though. I bet there wasn't one single newspaper or TV station that mentioned the fact that having been chased by riot police, several hundred English were literally imprisoned in a shit part of a shit town, unless we walked several miles with no guidance whatsoever from the pigs, which is what we ended up doing.

We walked down another road, in the opposite direction to the bridge, and took a right turn past the stadium. After about two miles, we asked another copper for directions, and then walked another mile before stopping a taxi which took us to the station. At last, we'd made it. After five hours, seven or eight miles walking and two miles in a taxi, we were on our way out of France's shittest World Cup venue. Fucking Northallerton could have handled the World Cup better, apart from Northallerton's ground doesn't hold 42,000.

At the station there were loads of English around, and a

few Colombians. We met the Huddersfield lot again from the other night in Paris, and they seemed quite pissed. They were a sound bunch and it was good to see some familiar faces after the shit day we'd had. We asked one of the station's staff when the next train to Lille was, but he advised us to get the train to Arras if we wanted to see the match, and then get a train to Lille after that.

The train finally came and we got to Arras about 20 minutes before kick off, and along with about 200 others we went looking for a bar. The first one was packed, and the rest were locking up when they saw us lot heading towards them. Wankers. If they want to lose money that's up to them. After about a ten minutes we finally found a bar that was open, just off the main square, and in the end there was about 100 English in there, ready for the match to start.

It was a decent bar, with TVs all over the place, and after getting the beers in I noticed that the restaurant side of the place was quite empty, and they had a few TVs in there. Seeing as we'd not eaten all day, we went through there and got a table. The waiter put a TV on for us which was in perfect view. Fucking sorted! After the day we'd had, I was in need of a skinful of beer, and promptly ordered another *grande biere* before deciding what to eat.

To follow on from the snails in Paris, Mel chose frogs' legs for a starter. Me and Matt went for something more normal and I ordered chicken for main course. And then it was time for the match to start. The singing started up next door, which we joined in with, and then we all stood up to sing along with 'God Save the Queen'.

Once the match started England were quickly in control. The atmosphere in the stadium sounded fucking brilliant as well, with England taking over the place. Shame we never had tickets, but at least I had a big glass of beer in front of me. One of the highlights was the French commentator, waffling on, and then he said, '*Et tout les supporters d'Angleterre chantez* "stand up if you hate Scotland".' Funny as fuck! Everyone laughed, cheered and joined in with the song. 'Stand up, if you hate Scotland!' Then I got back to my paté and salad. I tried one of Mel's frogs' legs, which didn't taste too bad but was all bones and tendons, so I chewed it and spat it out. Fucking frogs!

England were still playing well, looking safe at the back and dangerous up front. Then after about half way through the first half, Darren Anderton scored a great goal from just inside the area, launching the ball into the top of the net. The England players went mental, the England fans in the stadium went mental, next door went mental, and we went mental, jumping all over the restaurant area. Fucking yes! Quick swig of my beer, and then we joined in with the chant of 'One–nil to the En-g-land.'

About ten minutes later, England won a free kick just outside the area. I sat there saying, 'Top corner. Get ready to pick the ball out of the net keeper.' Up steps David Beckham and launches the ball over the wall and straight into the top corner. What a fucking great goal. Pick that one out you Spic bastards! Time to go mental again, jumping around the table.

It was soon half-time and England were cruising. The main course came which I soon scoffed down, and ordered another beer ready for the second half. It was great in that bar, with loads of English next door singing away, us and a few others sat eating and drinking at the tables, TVs all over the place, England winning, nice barmaid (there I go again), and the owner was a laugh as well, not being a daft twat like so many other bar owners in the town who were turning down trade. He must have doubled his week's takings that night.

In the second half we carried on as before, looking safe at the back, although we didn't create quite so many chances and failed to score again. The news came through that Tunisia were beating Romania 1–0. This would have put us top of the group on goal difference and we'd play Croatia in the Second Round instead of Argentina, with a possible Quarter Final against Germany. It was all suddenly going to plan, after the disappointment of the Romania match. But then the useless Arab cunts let in a late equaliser, and we're up against the Argies in St Etienne, instead of Croatia in Bordeaux. Oh well, we'd just have to win the World Cup the hard way, beating the Argies, the Dutch, Brazil and then the Germans in the Final. That was the plan anyway.

After the match, which ended 2–0, we were all happy as fuck and ended up going outside to join 50 or so others who left our pub and another nearby, and we were all repeating the scenes of Toulouse, jumping around and having a good celebratory sing-song. As we were stood there, we saw a familiar face. It was Hollis. We last saw him in Toulouse at the weekend, but somehow knew we'd see him again. We had a good laugh there, singing all the usual songs, plus 'Bring on the Argies, and people were leaning into passing cars and beeping the horns. It started getting out of hand though when a couple of dickheads started booting the cars and put a massive dent in one. There was no need for that. It's fair enough having a go at some foreign cunts who are up for it, but booting the cars of people driving past is pointless. So after a quick chat with Hollis, we decided to go back up to the station.

On the way up there a van full of riot police went past with its lights flashing. Then there was a bus full of the cunts. And another. And another, followed by three more and another van. Looks like we got out just in time. They probably went down to the square and nicked everyone there, no doubt including Hollis who was pissed out of his head. Foreign police like nothing better than a pissed-up Englishman making noise.

We got to the station and found out that the train wasn't due for another hour or so, so we stood around and talked to a Plymouth fan for a bit, who was lying on the floor and on the verge of passing out. He mentioned them lot beating us at Wembley in 1996, but didn't go on about it, which isn't surprising given that Argyle are back in Division Three after two shit seasons, plus the fact he was hardly capable of speaking.

So after that we went round to the front of the station and started talking to some Aldershot and Sunderland fans, as well as a few others, feeling happy after England's win. There were a load of others at the fountain about 50 yards away, singing away. They started a singing match with us when they sung 'Station, station give us a song, station, give us a song'. So I replied with a rendition of 'En-g-land, En-g-land, En-g-land...' which the others joined in with. This went on for a while until we were all fucked, so we went to the platform and waited for the train.

We got talking to some Millwall fans, and then the train came in about 20 minutes later. Me, Mel and Matt ended up sitting opposite the three Millwall lads, feeling knackered but still happy from the match. The train was fairly quiet apart from this irritating fucker with a St George's flag wig on, who just kept going on and on, walking up and down

Day 14, Friday 26 June

the carriage doing everyone's heads in. He told us he was from Great Yarmouth, but supported Liverpool not Norwich City, and went to 12 games last season. He disappeared and came back five minutes later, saying (in a Norfolk accent), 'Oi've just 'ad a smoke of some skunk, woite butterfloi from Amsterdam.' He then went down the carriage to annoy other people who were dozing off, saying, 'Wake up will you, we won didn't we, oi've just 'ad some woite butter-fly...' He said, 'On every train there's an irritating baastard, and on this train it's me.' What a twat!

His mate came and sat with us and started eating a pineapple, chopping it up with a knife and leaving a lovely sticky mess all over the floor. Fuck knows where he got that from. I think some Colombian had given it to him. He was pissed out of his head, but wasn't an irritating little fucker like his mate though.

As the train arrived back in Lille we went down to the end of the carriage, and started talking to three Sunderland fans who were there, all big fuckers. Then the Great Yarmouth wanker came along, saying, 'Oi'm from Great Yarmouth, Oi am, Oi've just smoked some woite butterfly.' One of the Mackems said to him (in a broad Sunderland accent), 'Just fuck off and sit down ya daft southern bastard before I fuckin' chin ya.'

We laughed at this, and Yarmouth looked a bit stunned at first, but then said, 'But Oi'm from the east country, Great Yarmouth, near Norwich,' to which the Mackem replied, 'Aye, I've been to Norwich and it's full of fucking wankers like you, now fuck off.' Yarmouth still went on, 'Oi'll sit down roight if you shake moi hand,' to which the response was, 'Just fuck off and sit down ya daft cunt.' He finally got the message and went back down the train. Daft twat, a

105

skinny 20-year-old pissing off three big fucking Mackems. We just laughed at the whole thing.

When we got off the train at Lille Flandres there were loads of police around, and the three of us walked down to the Lille Europe station where our bags were for the night. There were even more police down there and, as we queued to get into the station we even saw some British coppers there, which I have to say was quite a good sight after two weeks of the French police. It became apparent though that no one was allowed into the station unless they had a ticket for the Eurostar train that was leaving shortly, and the station wouldn't open again until 5.30 a.m., so we just sat on one of the benches outside, ready for a night of luxury.

I was physically and mentally tired, and had sobered up somewhat, but there was no way I was going to be sleeping that night. The three of us sat there, using our two flags as blankets, and watched the goings on around the station. There were quite a few people around for the first hour or so, until the Eurostar went at about 2.30 a.m. We saw someone wearing a Darlo shirt walking past, so we had a quick chat with him, seeing as he was the first other Darlo fan we'd noticed in France.

By 3 a.m., the police had gone and it was fairly quiet, and altogether there were about 20 of us sat there or lying there, using our flags to try and keep warm. But for the first time in two weeks I was cold. Fucking freezing in fact. A Man U fan came and sat with us, and a Cockney who was fairly quiet but I think was West Ham. The Man U fan was quite a good laugh, about 40 years old, and went to virtually every game, including all over Europe. He even lives in Manchester.

A few people came and went, including three lads from

London who supported Liverpool. One of them went off and sat in the middle of the road behind us, which seemed strange until we realised there was an air duct there, giving out warm air from the station down below. Another bloke walking around looked like a French train spotter, but he turned out to be English and had been to the match.

As it started getting light we were counting the minutes until the station opened. Even though the baggage office didn't open until 6.30 a.m., at least we could warm up a bit inside, and get a drink and something to eat. I didn't get a wink of sleep, but I think Mel and Matt maybe managed half an hour or so. I was well knackered, but knew I'd get a couple of hours' sleep on the train to Amsterdam, plus a few hours once we got there that afternoon. So 5.30 a.m. came and the station opened, and I suppose you could say that marked the start of another day...

Day 15, Saturday 27 June

So after a cold night outside the train station without getting any sleep, me, Matt and Mel went inside the train station, along with the 20-odd others that had spent the night outside, plus about another 50 people who'd turned up since 5 a.m. Once in there we found that the café didn't open until 6 a.m., and the bogs didn't open until 5.45 a.m., so I still couldn't have a piss and a coffee. We went along to the train information office to find out about trains to Amsterdam, and were advised to go to the Lille Flandres station.

On the way out of the information office the Man U fan who'd been sitting with us all night was leaving with one of the staff. He told us that he could get his bag out of the luggage office, because he was booked on to a train that was going before the office was due to open at 6.30 a.m. He said to go with him so we could get our bags, to save waiting around for another hour, so we did and got our bags out early.

After that the three of us went over to the other train station, feeling fucked due to no sleep, and went to check out the train times. There were a few other English asking for train times to Amsterdam, and we were told there was one just after 7 a.m., changing at Antwerp, so we had about an hour to spare. I went down to the bogs, but found they were closed, so had to wait a bit longer. As I was down there the police came along and woke up the remaining English that were sleeping there, being tossers by poking them with their batons, waiting for a reaction.

We waited for McDonalds to open, and then went in for breakfast. It was packed as fuck inside, especially with there being people like us wearing rucksacks. The staff didn't seem too happy with about 30 English lads in there, some of whom were trying their best to do the staff's heads in by being awkward. I was knackered and just got two egg muffins, black coffee and an orange juice for breakfast, followed by a long-awaited crap.

After that we went for the train to Antwerp, got on and sat down with a few other English who were scattered about on the train. Once we were on the move I soon dozed off, only awoken by the conductor announcing various stations along the way. The tannoy announcement signal was an irritating ding-ding-ding noise and, just to do my head in, Darlo have gone and installed the same thing at Feethams. Most of the other English got off somewhere in Belgium, and when I woke up again everyone around me was speaking Flemish or whatever it is they speak, some sort of variation of Dutch. I noticed one of the people in front was reading a newspaper, and the headline was all about 150 English trashing Ostend.

We got to Antwerp and waited for about 20 minutes for the train to Amsterdam. I was really struggling to keep my eyes open, but once on the train I soon fell asleep again. We were soon into Holland and going through Rotterdam, Den Haag (The Hague) and then into Amsterdam, by which time the train was quite full and I'd managed about another hour's sleep. I couldn't help noticing this gorgeous blonde bird that got on at Den Haag, but I was knackered and kept dozing off all the time. So it was now about 11.30 a.m. and we'd just arrived at Amsterdam.

On the way off we'd got talking to a lad from Colchester called Tom, who was on his own after being in Brussels with his mates, which he said had been a good laugh. We'd planned to stay at Camping Vlegenbos about a mile north of Central Station, where I'd stayed on my previous two visits to Amsterdam. They had log cabins there that only work out about a fiver a night each if there's four people, but we had tents if they were full. Tom decided to stay with us and get some accommodation sorted out.

As we walked out of Central Station an Australian bloke approached us on a mountain bike and asked us if we needed accommodation, and proceeded to go on and on about how wonderful the hotel was where he worked. It sounded okay though, £17 per night each, four in a room, only five minutes walk away, bar downstairs which stays open until 3 a.m., and a free first beer. I think it was the beer that swung it for me, plus the fact none of us could be bothered walking over a mile to the campsite, and I couldn't remember there being a bar there either.

So we went down to have a look at the hotel, and decided to take the room. It was nothing special but it was adequate, and after dumping our bags off we went down to the bar for a beer, and then off into town to get some money from the bureau de change. As I was waiting outside for the others some bloke came past and said, 'English, you want some coke, ecstasy?' I just ignored the twat. I was used to that sort of thing from being there before, and it does your head in at first but you soon get used to it. Matt then went back to the station with Tom, because he'd left his hat on the train – the one from the Madstock concert he'd been to a few months earlier. Me and Mel went back to the hotel for some beer, smelling the aroma of the coffee shops on the way. Welcome to Amsterdam!

Back at the hotel bar, me and Mel got the beers in and sat talking to the barman, who despite being Welsh was a fucking good laugh. He took the piss out of everyone and everyone took the piss out of him. There was a skinhead there as well, who was a right laugh. His name was Michel and he was French, but kept saying, 'I hate the fucking Frogs, but I am one. If I go there now they'll arrest me because they'll think I'm an English hooligan. But I hate the fucking French. 'Best Frenchman we'd met and he lived in Holland. For some reason I told him about Cardiff and showed him the scar on my head, and then he showed me where a Feyenoord fan had hit him on the head with a base-ball bat, thinking he was an Ajax fan. The bin incident in Cardiff must have been the most told story during the World Cup. From Southampton to Wolverhampton, from Manchester to Amsterdam, people will be saying, 'I met a Darlington fan who had a metal bin thrown on his head when he was having a shit at Cardiff!'

Matt and Tom returned after a while, but Matt didn't manage to find his hat. He was gutted, losing his Madness hat. So the four of us sat there, drinking away and talking to the Welsh barman and the French skinhead. Just to add a bit of international flavour, a middle-aged German biker came in, followed by an American doctor, and there were also a couple of Dutch in there. It was like the United Nations, all of us talking about all sorts of things. The Yank went on about some new treatment he'd created for bad backs, and ended up practising on Tom who had fucked his

111

back in a few months earlier. He was your typical loud mouth Yank who thought he knew everything. I know nothing about treating back pain though and he's a professional, so I just nodded in acknowledgement, and laughed at Michel who was taking the piss out of him.

By about 2.30 p.m. though I was feeling fucked, not through the booze but lack of sleep, so I went upstairs to crash out for a bit, as did Mel, while the other two went out for a wander around town. I soon fell asleep, and woke up several hours later. My watch said 8.30, but I didn't have a clue whether it was Saturday night or Sunday morning, as there was still the same grey sky outside. Matt and Tom had come back, and said it was still Saturday night, and Italy had beaten Norway 1–0.

Sound, time to go out for a night on the town. The four of us went down the road and stopped off at a bar just before Damrak, the main street that goes up to Central Station. We had a few beers in there, and watched the Brazil v Chile match, while listening to some banging tunes that they were pumping out. Brazil won 4–1, and the stereo system had fucked up, so we decided to go for a walk around the red light district.

We walked down Damrak and stopped off at McDonalds for something to eat. After that we headed for the canals where all the sex shops and windows were, and had a good look around. The sex shops have some unbelievable stuff in, most of it fucking disgusting. Titles such as *Fist fucker monthly* and *Golden shower* were quite common, then there's all the fucked-up stuff with animals, as well as the normal shagging and cock sucking (but unfortunately not just between men and women). I wonder what sort of sad cunt buys that shit.

So after a couple of sex shops we went down to where all the women were and had a good look at the whores in the windows. A lot of them were ugly as fuck, but some of them were fucking nice. Mind you they probably have about ten cocks up them a night. Going through those small side streets with women either side, everyone would keep bumping into the person in front, as they were too busy looking at the whores instead of where they were going.

There were loads of the usual tourists about, plus the odd group of English who kept on singing 'Vindaloo' and then there was all the wankers trying to sell coke or smack or shit like that. I was half expecting I'd have to hit some cunt who'd try and mug one of us, or get cocky when they're offering drugs, but there was no need.

Amsterdam's a fairly chilled-out place, although there's still plenty of dodgy cunts around. It made a nice break from France though, with no riot police waiting around every corner, or press out to report trouble. After the day in Lens, we just had to get away from the French (Michel in the hotel bar being the exception).

So after walking around the red light district for a while, we headed back to the hotel, where we sat in the bar for a bit drinking beer. None of the people who were there earlier were still there, just a fat Dutch bird behind the bar and a few ugly women with some soft-looking lads.

The four of us went upstairs to crash out, but a bunch of Yanks next door were playing shit music and were being loud-mouthed cunts. So I just put on the World Cup Special tape and crashed out, despite Tom snoring like fuck. I kept turning the tape up, especially when the Yank's music finished, and fell asleep shortly after our tape finished. The most appropriate song was 'The wall of orange', the chorus of which goes 'We're not going to the USA, but we don't wanna go there anyway' (referring to USA 94). The Yanks must have heard it.

Day 16, Sunday 28 June

We woke up to find that Tom had gone. I thought he must have gone down for breakfast, and took my turn in the shower. When the Australian bloke said that the room had a shower he was taking the fucking piss. There was no divider between the shower floor and the floor around the toilet, just a wooden board to stand on. And the water that came out was just a pathetic trickle. So the whole bathroom (if you can call it that) floor was flooded, but at least I was up and awake.

So I went downstairs to the bar ahead of the other two, and ordered my breakfast. As I sat down Michel was staring at me looking confused, and I said, 'All right mate.' He said, 'I know you...' and when I said, 'I was in here yesterday, we're staying upstairs,' he suddenly remembered who I was, and continued to roll his joint.

I ordered a beer to go with my breakfast, and the Welsh barman remembered he'd been given a note to give to me. It was from Tom. He'd left earlier when we were asleep, to get a flight back home as he had work the next day. He'd paid up his share for the room even though he only stayed for the one night. He was a good laugh and I think he'd enjoyed his brief visit to Amsterdam.

So along came my cooked breakfast which I soon ate, and then Mel and Matt came down and had some breakfast as well, while I sat there drinking beer. I tried to phone a hot-line number that the Football Association had set up in the event of there being extra tickets for the knockout stages. A message said that there were no extra tickets for the Argentina game, so I tried a few hotels in St Etienne from a guide book, but they were all full. We decided we'd go to Lyon and try to get a hotel there seeing as it's much bigger than St Etienne and was only an hour away on the train.

But we had more immediate things to think about, like a day in Amsterdam, so after shaking hands with Michel and Taffy, who wouldn't be in later, the three of us fucked off into town. The first thing we had to do was book a train down to Lyon for the next day, ahead of Tuesday's game against the Argies. So we went to Central Station and went to the booking and inquiries office. When we got there I had to take a ticket and wait for my number to show on one of the small screens, which took about 20 minutes. Once it was my turn we ended up getting booked on to the train that left at 8.25 a.m., and changed at Brussels and Paris Gare du Lyon, before arriving in Lyon at about 4 p.m.

After sorting that out we headed off down Damrak. We spent a few hours just wandering the streets and looking in various shops, before stopping off at McDonalds for lunch. We then looked around a few more shops, before deciding to look in the sex museum back up on Damrak.

We went into the torture museum just before that, and I was expecting it to be like the York Dungeons or London Dungeons, with loads of moving plastic models of people being sawn in half or having rats caged in on their stomach, eating their way through. But this one didn't have any models, just actual torture devices with diagrams next to them.

One of them was a wooden pyramid on top of a pole, and the victim was made to sit on top while weights were tied to his feet, pulling him down so the point of the pyramid would go right up his arse, splitting the poor fucker right up the middle. Fucking horrible. Mind you, given the sort of pornography in the sex shops, I wouldn't be surprised if there's a few sick cunts in Amsterdam who'd like to try it out on themselves.

Once we'd had a good look around at all the various torture equipment, we went a couple of doors up the road and into the sex museum. I'd been there before about six years earlier, but it had changed a lot since then. There's all sorts of pictures in there, and some little cubicles where people put money in for a video and presumably have a wank.

Upstairs they have loads of really old porn pictures, old black and white photos from the last century. Blokes with Victorian style tashes shagging some birds, and worst of all, there was an old photo of a woman being shagged by a fucking zebra. It got worse downstairs, in one room there were photos of men shagging sheep and cows, women being fucked by dogs, and men and women pissing all over each other. It was fucking unreal.

So after that little eye opener we went over the road and into a bar for a drink. I'd been there four years earlier and it hadn't really changed much. Then it was back to Damrak where we had dinner sat outside at a restaurant. Pizza and beer, nice start to the evening. Then it was back to another bar where we watched the football on a big screen between Denmark and Nigeria, although we got that fucked the football became a bit of a blur. Denmark won 4–1, which we were happy with but the two Nigerians at the bar weren't.

So we then went on another walk around the red light district, doing pretty much the same as the night before, looking in sex shops and looking at the whores, which did get quite tempting. Those streets around the canals all look the same though, especially when you're feeling fucked, and we just couldn't remember which way it was back to Damrak. We kept crossing bridges, walking one way, and then crossing over and walking back to where we'd been. We managed to find our way out in the end though, and went back to the Café Pollux, the hotel we were staying in.

After a quick beer the three of us went upstairs to bed. Couldn't be bothered putting any music on, but then the noisy bastard Yanks came in next door, being loud as fuck. I was lying there, trying to get to sleep, and all I could hear was, 'Oh my Gaad, I'm so stoned, how about you Braad...' On and on.

I didn't want to listen to them cunts gobbing on all night, so I said, loud as fuck and in my best Yorkshire accent, 'Shut the fuck up!' It worked a treat! They went quiet as fuck next door, just whispering the odd thing. They were probably saying, 'Jeez, it's those English soccer hooligans, we'd better be quiet or they might get pissed.' Daft fuckers. Mel vowed to wake them up in the morning, seeing as we were getting a 7 a.m. alarm call.

Day 17, Monday 29 June

We got up after our early morning knock on the door, soaked the bathroom with that shit shower, and then we were ready to leave. As we left though, Mel steamed into the crappy door that joined our room with the Yanks next door, making a right fucking noise. I thought the door was going to go through, but it never. It must have woke the cunts up though.

After leaving the hotel we went straight up to Central Station and waited for our train, which arrived within about 15 minutes. We didn't have reservations for that train so just got on and took over a free compartment, dumping one of our rucksacks on the seats rather than the luggage racks. As people came on the train afterwards an American women came past looking for seats, followed by her two young girls. Even though there was eight seats in there, only three of us and one rucksack on a seat, after one look at us, the two kids were saying, 'Mommy, Mommy, there's no seats in there, Mommy, Mommy.' In their eyes, I suppose we were rough English hooligans who wanted to cause trouble.

But their mum said there was enough room and asked Matt politely to move his rucksack, which he did, so we were sharing the compartment with them. She was okay, just thick as fuck when it comes to life outside of the USA (aren't all Americans like that?), while her two daughters were quiet as fuck, which is just as well because my head wasn't in the best of conditions.

The Yank started talking to us, and when we said we were there for the football, she said, 'Oh my gaad, we've been told to watch out for you guys.' She then went on to say, 'What's England's offence like?' and asked why police are expecting trouble at the England v Argentina game. I said something about the Argies not liking the fact that we beat them in the Falklands War, and that football means a lot to people outside of America, but didn't go on too much about the Argies being greasy Spic scum who need a kicking because of the two kids being there.

But the worst thing was when she asked, 'Didn't you guys build a canal between England and France?' Thick bitch! We explained that there's been a channel over 25 miles across for millions of years, and we've recently built a tunnel under it. Fucking Yanks wouldn't notice a world war until it hit the USA (didn't that happen last time?).

A big woman conductor came along and interrupted our interesting conversation with the USA's *Mastermind* champion, and asked for our tickets. When we showed her our inter-rail passes and reservations she said that our tickets were for second class and we were sat in first class, and we would have to move. If that shit carriage was first class, fuck knows what the rest of the train was like. She went off down the carriage and we just stayed there.

About ten minutes later she came back though and, upon seeing us in her precious excuse for a first class compartment, she shouted out, 'I thought I told you to do something, now do it.' Rather than argue with a 16-stone woman mud wrestler in front of kids we left the carriage and sat round the corner, on those shit pull-down seats by the door.

There was another Yank there who had suffered the same fate as us.

So we sat there for the next hour or so until the train got to Brussels. The American family got off at Antwerp, and the woman made various references to the 'iron lady', as she called her. Once we got to Brussels we got straight on to the train to Paris Gare du Lyon, and found our reserved seats. This train was much better, and we were in the smoking compartment as well. Once we were moving I went to the buffet carriage next door, and bought a sandwich and a couple of beers for breakfast. I got talking to a Geordie in there, who thought that St Etienne was near Paris, and started moaning when I said it was another two or three hours away. I went back to my seat and the Geordie came with us, but left after moaning about the smoke. Bit of a whingeing cunt really.

When we got to Paris we had about an hour to spare, so we left the station to find a café or something to get some lunch. We found a small café near the station, and each got a roast chicken sandwich, which was tasty as fuck. The only thing that spoilt it was when some workmen pulled up in a truck, poured a load of tarmac or bitumen on the pavement outside, and fucked off. It made a right fucking stink and put me off my food. Wankers.

We left there and headed back to the station, making a quick phone call home on the way. Once at the station we waited around for the platform to be announced, and then went for the train after I'd bought a *Daily Telegraph*. I'd been missing that paper, as the only English papers I'd seen in France were the shitty tabloids, other than *The Times* that I'd bought in Toulouse.

Our train was one of the TGV trains, and when I got to

our seats I found an Argie sitting there, sprawled out and half asleep. I knocked his foot as I sat down, and he opened his eyes, saw my England hat and mumbled some Spic shit that ended in *Inglesi*. I stared at him and told him to shift his foot. When Matt sat down next to him he knocked the Argie's elbow off the arm rest, and when the Spic mumbled something, Matt said, 'What's your problem mate?' No response. Once me, Matt and Mel were sat down, a nice-looking French lass came along and said Matt was in her seat, which meant the Argie was in Matt's seat. 'Oi mate, you're in his seat.' Then one of the Argie's mates opposite said, 'Hey, Alejandro...' (Spic waffle), and the twat moved to sit with his greasy mates.

I thought we were gonna end up fighting on the train with four Argies, even before St Etienne, but that French bird sitting there seemed to calm down the feelings of Anglo-Argie hatred. She was certainly a much better sight to look at. We were soon on the move and I settled down to reading the *Daily Telegraph*, which had an article in that quoted Cecil Rhodes, 'to be born English is to win the lottery of life'. To be born an Argie is to forget to put your money on. The rest of the journey was fairly uneventful, other than hearing Spic music coming out of a Spic walkman, as well as the odd glimpse at the French bird's tits. But unfortunately it was nothing like the train down to Marseilles, and there seemed to be hardly any English on board.

We got to Lyon at about half past four, and found that it was as hot as fuck. First stop was the tourist office at the station, but we couldn't find one, so we walked out of the station in the search for accommodation. Not again, was the general feeling. After walking around aimlessly for half an hour, we found a big hotel right next to the station, which although was quite posh for our standards and quite expensive, was decent enough and in a good location, and Mel had enough credit left on his card, so we decided to check in there. The receptionist said they only had enough room for one night, but might have another one after 11 a.m. the next morning. The room only had two beds, but Matt said he'd sleep on the floor if he could pay a bit less.

We turned the TV on to find that Mexico were beating Germany 1–0, with about half an hour left. Fucking brilliant! Matt said that Germany were bound to come back and win it. Sure enough, 20 seconds later, the bastards equalise, fucking Klinsmann. I hate that cunt. Fair enough, he's a good player, but he just sums up the cockiness of the German team over the last ten years, and he dives like a poof when anyone goes near him. Plus the fact he played for Tottenham. But then, ten minutes later, the bastards go and score again and win 2–1. Oh well, at least we'd still have the satisfaction of beating them later on in the tournament.

After the football finished we decided to go out and get something to eat, as well as the obligatory getting pissed. There was an Irish pub right next door, which was effectively part of the train station, so we went in there, knowing that it would be full of English. It was quite smart in there, well done out, a few English about, not many others, and the best thing was that they had pint glasses and staff that were either English, Irish or spoke good English. So we got three pints in, and I was already off for my second pint by the time the other two had made any sort of an impression on theirs. I was in the mood for getting pissed.

The three of us got something to eat, which was good quality stuff, and then spent the night drinking pint after pint of lager. We decided that after England beat the Argies, we'd go to Grenoble and go up into the Alps for a few days to chill out, before returning to the madness of Marseilles for the quarter final against Holland (they'd just beaten Yugoslavia while we were in the pub). After that we'd go home because our rail passes ran out on that day. That was the plan anyway.

It was a good laugh in there, although the atmosphere wasn't quite the same as it had been before the other England games. But after getting pissed and talking about all sorts, including making up a Darlo version of the 'Vindaloo' song, we headed off back to the hotel to crash out. The plan for the next day was to check out train times to and from St Etienne and watch the match there if possible, either at the stadium if we could get a ticket cheap enough or in a bar down there. Failing that we'd just watch the match in a bar in Lyon.

Day 18, Tuesday 30 June

I had some weird dreams before waking up, but the one that stuck in my head was when I dreamt that I was tied up next to someone who got shot in the head, with blood flying everywhere. Then it was my turn, but I managed to wake up just in time. I was fucking freaked out when I woke up, and as I sat looking out of the hotel window, Mel said I looked gutted and asked what was up. I said I'd just dreamt that I'd been shot in the head, but was hungover as well. The worst thing was reading the news on Ceefax when I got home, to see the headline 'Two people shot in head in separate incidents', and it happened the night I had the dream. Fucking weird!

Anyway, back to the World Cup, and despite a spooky start to the day, I was looking forward to England getting revenge over Argentina, after the cheating bastards beat us in the 1986 World Cup in Mexico, with that wanker Dago Maradona scoring with his hand. Hand of God my arse. Hand of a cheating Spic more like. I was confident that England were going to stuff Argentina, on the way to winning the World Cup.

Me and Mel went down to reception to see if they had any rooms for that night. They said to come back in half an hour, and when we did they said that our room was free, so we took our bags back up there and went to the station.

We found out that there were trains back to Lyon from St Etienne until about midnight, so we decided to go there and watch the match, especially as it was less than an hour away on the train.

The train was mostly full of English, but there was the odd small group of Argies there as well ('There's Diego and his friends,' said someone as we got on the train). The journey itself was quite boring, although I was sat opposite someone in some sort of a Shakespearean type fancy dress costume, which I couldn't stop grinning at.

Once at St Etienne we went across the road to a bar, where we got a beer each. We wanted something to eat but Mel had seen a dog walking all over the food counter so we didn't bother. Dirty cunts! So after checking with a local sitting near us that the town centre was up over the top of the hill, we set off to find another bar where we could get something to eat.

There were quite a few other English about, but not so many Argies, and we found a bar after walking for about 15 minutes, just up from the town centre. There were quite a few English in there, all drinking beer and eating steak and chips, and we decided to do the same. There was only one person working in there, and it took us ages to get served, but although the food wasn't anything special, it was worth waiting for. It'd be a good beer base for the day anyway. Most of the people seemed to be Chelsea fans in there, and I'd say that we'd seen more Chelsea than anyone else in France. Most England fans over there seemed to be from London, the West Midlands or West Yorkshire, although every part of the country was represented, even Darlo, York and Hartlepool Scum.

After our beer, steak and chips we went further down the

road to the town centre, and sat around in the square where the town hall is. This square was smaller and greener than the one in Toulouse, and there was about twice as many English as Argies there. Everyone was just sat around chilling out, drinking beer and enjoying the sun. There were dozens of people walking around with bits of cardboard, which had 'I need a ticket / *je cherche pour une billet*' written on, just like there was in Lens but on a bigger scale. No one seemed to have any luck though. We expected to end up watching the match in a bar somewhere, but said we'd try down near the stadium for some tickets before the match. The FA had only been allocated 2,000 tickets for this match, but they had agreed to this allocation two years ago and knew the score, so they couldn't out of it that easily.

Kick off was another seven hours away, so we went across the road for some beers, and sat outside for a while, watching the various goings on. Not very exciting, just people drinking or looking for tickets. There wasn't any hint of trouble like the media had been suggesting, although it was still early. When I came out of the bar after getting another drink, Mel and Matt were on the curb outside pretending to beg, with Mel holding his hat out in a begging gesture as people walked past. Some old French bloke chucked some money in and then said, 'Non, non, viens avec moi,' and took the three of us into the bar for a beer.

The old bloke must have been well into his seventies, and didn't speak a word of English, but he bought us all a beer. He said he was Polish, and spoke French, German, Czech, Russian and of course Polish, which made his French hard as fuck to understand. He did like the fact that I spoke French and German though, and went on to say how he liked the English, but thought the Scottish are weird because the men wore skirts. We just had to agree. I offered to get the next round in, but he insisted on buying them, so we had another free beer.

We got bored with the old bloke after a while, and decided to find another bar. He still wanted to buy us beer somewhere else, but we just walked off ahead of him after thanking him for the beers. We found another square down the road where they had a band on, and the Romania v Croatia match would be shown on the big screen there shortly. The square was packed with English, with flags tied up around the fences, and we went to the bar for a beer. After a while Matt and Mel went off to watch the football on the big screen, but I stayed around the bar to get pissed.

I sat down at one of the tables and talked to some Bolton and Oxford fans, plus a few others. So I ended up getting quite pissed, sat there for the next hour and a half. While I was there it nearly went off when some Argies walked past and some English chucked a couple of chairs at them, but it was all over in a few seconds. I didn't see how it started, but it was nothing really, probably just one of the Argies mouthing off. Mel and Matt came back at half time, but disappeared for the second half. I couldn't be bothered standing in front of a screen watching a shit match, although I ended up going there for the last five minutes.

Croatia won that match 1–0, and with over two hours before the England match kicked off, we decided to make our way down to the stadium to see if there were any tickets going. I was quite pissed by this stage, and on the way down a kid who was only about 11 or 12 asked us for a light for his cigarette (*Avez vous un feu?*), and I just told him to fuck off. Poor little fucker probably shit himself, but he shouldn't be smoking at that age. When we got down to near the stadium, we found that the police had closed off the streets, only letting ticket holders past, and there didn't seem to be many tickets on sale.

So we just sat in a bar and spoke to some French for a bit, mainly just *'Angleterre va gagner le coupe du monde'*. We then got talking to some Barnet fans, who were quite a good laugh, before deciding to get a bus back up to the station where we could find a bar and watch the match, seeing as we had no chance of getting a ticket for any sort of decent price. We went round the corner and got on a bus that took us up to the train station, which only took about five minutes.

There were loads of English there, and we ended up sitting on the roundabout for a while, drinking, smoking and talking to some others there. We got talking to a West Ham fan called Steve, who was a good laugh. He had no front teeth, and said, 'ICF mate. Naa, I'm too old for the fighting now though, I'm 32, I just leave that to you lot.' He pointed to the sky and said, 'Me mum's up there, her and Bobby Moore, side by side.' There were a few Millwall there as well who Steve ICF seemed to know, and after talking to them we went off to find a bar to watch the match in. The one we'd just bought beers in wasn't letting anyone else in, and they wouldn't put the football on in the other room, so we told them to fuck off and walked up the road a bit, before finding a bar that wasn't too packed and was showing the football.

We got the beers in and found a table and seats at the front, which meant having to constantly look up to see the screen. The place soon filled up with other English, so we couldn't complain really. So with beer in front of us, about 60 other English around us, and confidence flying high, we were ready for the match to begin. England v Argentina, World Cup Second Round. This was it. Come on England!

There was a good atmosphere in there, and we all stood up to sing along to 'God Save the Queen'. Once the match started, Argentina cheated and got a dodgy penalty, which they scored. Bastards. But then five minutes later England equalised with an equally dodgy penalty, although ours was more of a penalty than theirs. We all went mental when Shearer put the ball in the net, and there was plenty of singing in there, especially the usual 'En-g-land, En-g-land, En-g-land...' as well as the familiar *Great Escape* theme tune, which we could hear on the TV as well.

England were playing really well and were looking like potential world champions. After about half an hour, Michael Owen got the ball just inside the Argies' half, and went on one of his runs. He beat a couple of defenders, kept going, got inside the area and launched an unstoppable shot into the top corner. YYYeeeeeeaasss! What a fucking goal! Maradona eat your heart out. Fucking magic! The pub went mental, celebrating Owen's goal that put us 2–1 up. Definitely the best goal of the World Cup.

England nearly got a third goal when Scholes missed an easy chance. But as we were singing away, expecting England to walk away with it, one of the Argie players dives like a poof and the shit ref gives them a free kick just outside the area. Instead of shooting, the sly bastards pass the ball to the side of the wall, leaving one of their players to put the ball in. 2–2. Bollocks. And that's how it stayed until half time.

Once the second half was underway, England carried on as before and looked likely winners. But then David Beckham gets fouled and as he's lying on the floor he kicks out at the Argie that just fouled him, who dives as if he's just been knee-capped. But all the players were told over and over again before the tournament about not retaliating to incidents, so Beckham was a stupid twat for doing what he did. The twat ref sends Beckham off, so we're down to ten men with over half an hour left. England play well though and never really looked threatened, soaking up the pressure well.

With just a few minutes remaining the ball is crossed in to the Argie area and Sol Campbell jumps up to head it in at the far post. Surely the winner, and it was time to go mental again. But no, the fucking twat referee disallows the goal, apparently saying that Shearer fouled the keeper when he jumped up to try and get the ball. That's bollocks. There was fuck all wrong with that goal so we won fair and square.

Not according to the ref though, so we had to have extra time with the golden goal rule (first goal wins). Despite being robbed England continue to play well, and should have had a penalty when an Argie defender blatantly handled the ball in their penalty area, but the stupid Danish cunt referee didn't give it. It's that fucking hand of God again. So, after having a dodgy penalty and dodgy free kick awarded against us, Beckham sent off for a yellow card offence after the Spic dived, Campbell being denied a legitimate goal, and the hand of God appearing again, it was down to penalties.

Even though England went out of Euro 96 and Italia 90 on penalties, we were all confident that we'd win this, seeing as it was England's destiny to win the World Cup. Both teams scored their first penalty, but then Argentina missed their second and we were celebrating. But Paul Ince misses England's next one and it was all level. Bollocks. Still confident though. The next few penalties all went in, with each of England's being met with a cheer and a fist in the air. Soon it was 4–3 to Argentina, and David Batty was stepping up to take England's last of the five penalties before sudden death. I was feeling nervous, knowing that he had to score to keep us in the Cup. Batty shoots, and the keeper saved it. NNNOOOOO! No fucking way. That was it. England out of the World Cup.

FUCK, FUCK.

I just couldn't believe it. The bar went silent, everyone looking around in disbelief or holding their heads in their hands. 'They can't do that,' I said, 'that's our World Cup. We were gonna win that.' We were so gutted. The disbelief and disappointment soon turned to anger. 'The cheating Argie bastards. I'm not leaving this town until I've done a fucking Argie.' The TV was turned off and we went outside.

Three weeks of being treated like shit by the French authorities, being labelled scum by our own press, and being cheated out of the World Cup again by the Argies just took over, and I was fucking mad. People were walking around, looking for Argies. Mel said we should go back to the station, and that there was no point in getting nicked. 'No, I'm not leaving this town until I've done an Argie,' I replied. Matt was feeling mad as well.

We were walking slowly up the road, away from the station, with a few others, looking for an excuse to kick off. Just then a car goes past beeping their horn like a twat, taking the piss out of us. Mel suddenly ran after the cunt, shouting, 'Come on.' I didn't waste any time and took off after him, determined to get the cunt out of the car and beat the shit out of him. The car had stopped at some traffic lights so we had a chance, but as I ran underneath a signpost supported by two posts, I ran into one of the posts and cracked my elbow. 'Fuck,' I said, before resuming the chase and shouting, 'Come on you fucker.' The twat must have seen us and realised he was going to get a kicking, so he pulled out from behind a couple of other cars and jumped a red light to get away from us. Unfortunately he didn't crash and disappeared around the corner. Bastard.

We went back to where Matt was and decided to head back down to the station. There wasn't much going on, other than a couple of bottles being thrown at parked cars, and we didn't want to miss our train back to Lyon. When we got down to the station there was a shit load of police and train station staff around, and they asked to see our tickets before letting us into the train station. Once in there we checked the train times and found we had about 20 minutes to wait, so we went back outside and I smoked a tab. We went back into the station a few minutes later, but one of the station's staff asked me for my ticket. I was fucking pissed off and just said, 'Fuck off, I've just fucking shown you it,' and barged past the cunt. The phrase, 'We're a right set of bastards when we lose' springs to mind.

The station was full of English, totally pissed off, deva- stated, gutted, subdued, numb, empty, frustrated, dejected, depressed. Words just can't explain how gutted we were. It was the end of the dream. The end of the holiday. When Germany beat us on penalties in Euro 96, I tried to console myself by saying, 'Fucking European Championship. It's shit. We'll just win the World Cup instead.' So I'd spent the last two years convinced that England were going to win the World Cup, but now it was all over.

Once on the train I sat down and accidentally knocked some Japanese-looking Frog who was dozing off. He mumbled something and I said, 'You what, you French cunt?' He just shook his head and I realised there was no point in taking out my frustration on him. He turned out to be okay and offered his cigarettes around a few times.

The train was almost silent, full of glum-looking faces. Steve ICF appears, and bursts into a chorus of 'I'm for ever blowing bubbles', West Ham's song. That put the spirit back into me, and I felt much better, saying, 'At least we're English,' and singing, 'English, and we're proud of it.' Steve was your stereotypical cockney and was just what was needed to lift our spirits. It didn't have a very long-lasting effect though, as nothing could take our minds away from being knocked out of the World Cup on penalties. Again. By Argentina. 'Oh well, only another six weeks and we'll be watching Darlo again,' I said.

The train journey became boring after a while, and for some reason stopped in the outskirts of Lyon for no apparent reason. We were there for about 15 minutes, and after shouting out of the window 'Move the fucking train,' I burnt some paper towels that were on the floor for something to do. I must have been feeling a bit destructive, although it just left a pile of ash and made a stink.

There was another Japanese-looking Frog opposite who was fast asleep, and nothing we tried doing would wake him up. People tried prodding him, taking his shoes off and chucking them at him, but he still wouldn't wake up. Mel said I should set fire to his hair, but after giving an insane grin, I sat back and said, 'No way, 'cos I would.' I'm not that fucking stupid though, it was just a funny idea.

The train finally pulled in to Lyon station, and we got off the train to the usual greeting of riot police. At least we wouldn't be seeing much more of them. I could've done with a drink, but the pub next to the station was closed, so we went back to the hotel and raided the mini-bar in the room, replacing vodka with tap water and not marking it on the card.

So that was it. Out of the World Cup. Sat in the hotel room, totally gutted. At least we'd had a good holiday though. We talked about what to do in the morning, and concluded that going home would be the best option, although we'd decide for definite in the morning. We were sick of France.

Day 19, Wednesday 1 July

Within a few seconds of waking up, I realised that England were out of the World Cup. 'Bollocks. Fucking cheating Argie scum,' were my first words of the day. Once we were all awake, we decided that we should go home. Our moods hadn't really changed much from the night before. We could have gone to Amsterdam again, but we were just so gutted that we wanted to go back to good old England. So we left the hotel and went down to the train station.

Once at the station we went to find out the train times, and found that there was a train straight through to Lille in about 15 minutes. It was a TGV train, so after buying some breakfast we went to buy our reservation tickets. There were quite a few Croatians around, ready for their quarter-final against Germany at the weekend, and a couple of Argies, but mostly pissed-off-looking English. The queues for tickets were massive though, and just as I got near to the front of one queue, the counter closed. Bastards. We'd just have to get our reservation tickets on the train, so we went up to the platform to wait for the train.

When the train came in we sat on the pull-down seats at the end of a carriage, seeing as we had no seats reserved. The journey was quite boring at first and we had four hours ahead of us. There were some Man City fans just through the door into the carriage, and one of them was showing everyone his picture in a book called *The Guvnors,* all about City's firm in the 1980s.

The conductor came down after a while, and after showing him our inter-rail tickets he said we had to pay a 60 franc supplement, even though it would have been 20 francs if we'd bought it at the train station. We told him that there was no time to buy one at the station, but he insisted that we pay 60 francs. One of the Man City fans went past and the conductor asked for his ticket, and when he saw the ticket he said, 'That's not your ticket,' but the City fan just walked off. Matt continued arguing with the conductor, and then the French cunt just said, 'Okay, I call the police at the next station,' and walked off in a huff. What a wanker.

We thought nothing of his threat, expecting maybe a couple of coppers to get on the train somewhere. But an hour later the train pulled into a station near Paris, and there must have been about a hundred riot police and SNCF security guards waiting on the platform. They came on asking for tickets, and the three of us showed our inter-rail tickets, but they never asked for the supplement. But the cunts grabbed hold of four of the Man City fans and dragged them off the train, threw them on the platform face down, and handcuffed them. They'd done fuck all apart from one or two maybe had dodgy tickets, and had just been having a beer.

A French woman in her fifties protested to the guards at the way the City fans were being treated, and one of the cunts raised his baton and was about to hit her, until one of the others restrained him. Fucking wanker, threatening to hit a defenceless woman with a young child. These cunts were well out of order.

After a while one of the lads who was dragged off

was allowed back on. Apparently they'd put him in the back of a van, breathalised him, and let him go. One of the ones not let back on hadn't even had a drink that day, but they arrested him for being pissed. What the fuck were they playing at? They're train passengers, not car drivers. A couple of people without tickets and three others arguing over the supplement does not warrant 100 riot police and security guards to get on the train, who then act like the scum of the earth. That would never happen in England.

After waiting half an hour for fuck all, the train finally got moving. One of the City fans, a big black lad in his late thirties, was talking to the French woman who nearly got hit. She said she was disgusted at the way the coppers and guards acted, and was ashamed to be French. The City fan said, 'Luv, if he'd hit you, with your little bambino next to ya, it would have gone off on here, ya know what I'm saying.' Fucking right! French bastards. She rightly pointed out that we would have been playing their game, that they wanted a reaction.

The conductor came back with his army of guards, and asked the City fan that had been dragged off for his ticket. He said he had his passport, but the ticket was taken off him with another load of papers when he was pinned down on the platform. It took about three attempts for them to understand that he didn't have a ticket because the riot police nicked a book with all his papers in.

The black City fan asked the guard why he was going to hit the French woman. Of course, the soft French bastard just said that he didn't understand. Lying cunt. He was well out of order, and the French woman said she would make a complaint. For the rest of the journey up to Lille, we sat opposite the remaining two City fans. They were sound lads, and had done fuck all to get arrested. One of them said to the French woman, 'Luv, after what's happened here, Anglo-French relations ... down the pan.'

As the train pulled in to Lille, I couldn't help noticing how small and soft a couple of the guards looked. So I said, 'How the fuck can a soft cunt like that be a security guard?' It was tempting to kick off on them, but you never know who's going to back you up, plus they had batons, and would have riot police there in no time. At least we never had to pay the supplement.

Once in the station, we decided to check out how much the Eurostar to London would be. We'd never been through the Channel Tunnel before, and it would save a couple of hours' travelling time. It was only about a 350-francs supplement using our inter-rail passes, so we booked on to the train and waited around for an hour or so.

Mel went into the shop to use up his change, and get me a *Weekly Telegraph*, a tabloid-size *Telegraph* that's only available abroad. Me and Matt missed out on a funny sight though, as Mel said he'd fallen over on his back in there, and couldn't get up at first because of his rucksack, and was lying there like a turtle, waving his arms and legs. A lass that'd been on the train had seen him, and said it was well funny.

After going through passport control we went down to wait for the train, whistling 'The Great Escape' on the way. We felt so glad to be on our way back to England, although we'd had a brilliant time in France. Once the train came in we found our seats and I sat and read the *Telegraph*. We were soon on the move, and I went to the buffet car next door to get some beers. We stopped at the Calais station that we should've gone to a few weeks earlier. It was in the middle of nowhere, so it's no wonder we didn't find it.

The tunnel itself was just like any other tunnel, but obviously much longer. The strange thing was that I didn't notice us going down very much, it was more of a constant slope. We cheered once we came out at the other side, back in good old Blighty! Bye bye France, hello England.

The three of us sat there reflecting over the past few weeks, and decided to have some awards. There were things like Best Character We'd Met (Hollis), Best Service (the Indian in Paris), Best Frenchman (Michel in Amsterdam), Worst Keeper (Jim Leighton), Best Goal (Michael Owen v Argentina). The full list is in Appendix One at the back of the book.

We soon arrived at Waterloo ('me and me mate and me cousin, we're off to Waterloo, me and me mate and me cousin with a bucket of Vindaloo!'), and went through customs to the Underground. After checking train times I phoned home to arrange a lift, and we got the tube up to King's Cross. Me and Mel went to buy some beer for the train in the shop just outside King's Cross station. As we crossed the road we realised that we were looking the wrong way, having got used to traffic being on the right. We didn't have a clue.

So after buying our beer and saying farewell to Matt, we went along the platform and got into the smoking carriage. The next two and a half hours was spent drinking beer and talking about our time in France. England away is fucking brilliant, and we'd decided to go to the first Euro 2000 qualifier in Sweden in September. The disappointment of being out of the World Cup had faded a bit, as we talked about what a great time we'd had. Much better than sitting home and watching it on TV.

Once back at Northallerton, I got a lift home, dropping Mel off on the way, and told my parents about what I'd been up to. It must have been quiet for them, with me in France, my brother Barney in the Bahamas and my other brother Dan living in York. I couldn't believe it when they said that they'd watched the football and were getting well into it, seeing as they usually hate football and even got married on World Cup Final day 1966. My dad even said that he would've gone to the pub to watch the next match, if we'd got through.

So that was it, back home early, out of the World Cup. I was too knackered to go to the pub that night, but I'd have plenty of time to tell everyone all about it. Roll on the new season!

Conclusion

What a fucking great time we'd had! Although I was gutted that we were out of the World Cup, the fact that I'd been over there and had the best holiday ever seemed to make things not seem so bad. I had loads of stories to tell everyone, and loads of photos to show. I'd got some good photos in Toulouse when we were all dancing around the square.

There are many highlights of our time at the World Cup, but I'd say the best moments were both nights in Marseilles and the weekend in Toulouse. The train down to Marseilles is a good memory, and that night in the bar near the hotel was brilliant. But the best piss up and singsong had to be in Toulouse, from the London Town pub to the main square.

We'd met some sound people in France, and the feeling of being abroad watching England is brilliant. Everyone's there for a laugh, they love their country, love football, love getting pissed. I sort of felt at home among that lot. England United. It seems that supporting England is one of the few ways you can express your love for the country without being called racist.

I'm fucking sick of politically correct wankers saying what's racist and xenophobic. While I've slagged a few people off in my book with a few stereotypes, I'm not racist. I just say what I like and am politically incorrect. Being patriotic does not mean that I am racist. I love my country, but I don't hate others (although parts of this book may imply otherwise!). A married man loves his wife, and she's special to him, but he doesn't hate all other men's wives. It may sound like a strange comparison, but it's the same principle.

And these twats that are offended by the Union Jack need their heads testing. Saying it's a racist symbol. So why do black athletes wave the flag with pride when they've won a race for Britain? What do these do-gooders think then? The Union Jack is the flag of the United Kingdom, and anyone that doesn't like it can fuck off. Personally I prefer the St George's flag though, because I consider myself to be English before anything else.

Another thing I've concluded from nearly three weeks in France is that the European Union will never work. There's no way I want them cunts on the train arresting me, or the French authorities having any say in my life, especially when it comes to football. I've been strongly against the EU for years, because it's undemocratic, wasteful, and no one has ever given them the right to rule our country. How can anyone say that something is EU funded when the UK is a net contributor to the EU budget? We just get a small refund of our own money. Our politicians are lying to us, even though on the continent all politicians openly admit that the idea of Economic and Monetary Union is to achieve political union in Europe.

So unless you want the UK to be broken up and become small provinces of Euroland, don't vote for the Single Currency, no matter what propaganda our soft government gives out. The people of Europe are too different to be one state. We should be friends and co-operate on international issues, maintaining economic and political independence, but not create a utopian super-state that will end in another war. No one wants it apart from deceitful politicians.

Moving away from politics, I have to say that I'm disgusted with the way the press reported events in France. Calling us scum and a disgrace. It's as if they were sat in their office in London writing the stories. They see a mob of English, something happens, and they say 'English thugs go on rampage' or some shit like that. And the politicians are no better, apart from that Alan Clark who stuck up for us, and he got slated for that. Mind you, as much I have slagged off *The Sun*, at least they're against the Single Currency.

Someone at work had the *Daily Mail* one day in September, and there was a report about a video by a thug that glorifies the violence of the World Cup and is a total disgrace. So I bought the video, called *Teargas and Tantrums*, by Eddy Brimson, and I thought it's quite good. In no way does he glorify the violence, he's not a thug (that's the impression from the video anyway, I don't know about his numerous books though), he's just an ordinary football fan following England around France for the World Cup. He shows the real events in Marseilles, and makes the viewer aware of the disgusting treatment of the English by the riot police (although the video does get repetitive after a while with the picture of his face continually saying 'It's a bit naughty' or 'I dunno if I'll get in'). As Sven had told me, on the beach at Marseilles the Tunisians were throwing missiles at the English (including families) and the police responded by standing next to the Tunisians and tear-gassing the English.

If the *Daily Mail* really believes that the video is glorifying violence and Eddy Brimson is a mindless thug, I seriously have to ask the question: What fucking planet are they and all other media wankers living on? Certainly not this one. It's a fucking disgrace, and I certainly recommend the video to anyone who wants to know what it was really like to be at the World Cup. This book and that video are the truth behind France 98, never mind all the sensationalist shite that was in the media.

Back to more positive things, me, Matt and Mel went out to Sweden for the qualifier, which England lost 2–1. On the train down to London, me and Mel made up a version of the Bobby Sands chicken supper song for Matt and his chicken korma. We had a great time, and just knew we'd see Hollis, and sure enough, there he was as soon as we walked out into the stadium. Hollis said that he wasn't arrested in Arras like we thought, but he'd got back into the bar and was there until 5 a.m. He was there with Kerry, his soon to be wife, and said that when they get married he's going to get the organist to play 'The Great Escape'. The women in Sweden are absolutely stunning, although the beer's a bit expensive.

On the first night over there we went to a bar near our hotel (which was miles from anywhere), and got pissed for several hours after having some food. Nice barmaid (there I go again) called Petra from Finland. We got talking to two big bastards who were also from Finland, and they were a great laugh. One of them said, 'We're from Finland, we hate the fucking Swedish,' followed by, 'If you fight tonight, we fight with you, we back you up.' They even paid our bill of about £25, so they must like English football fans. The Swedes in the bar started singing after a while, including a fucked-up version of 'The Great Escape', so the three of us responded with 'God Save the Queen' and 'No Surrender', followed by 'Stand Up if You Hate Man U' (which the two Finns joined in with).

We walked around Stockholm for most of the next day, stopping in loads of different bars. At one point we were sat outside a bar in a narrow side street, with about a dozen other English on the tables behind us along the side of the street. As we were talking about something or other a fat Swedish bloke in military uniform walks past us all, red faced and puffing away. He looked like the Michelin man in an army uniform, and after the three of us creased up laughing, every other England fan burst out laughing as they saw this bloke walk past, the laughter passing along the tables like a domino effect, and carrying on long after he'd gone. He must have felt awful, but it was just one of those moments when you can't help but laugh.

After a few more beers we went off to the stadium, the scene of our Euro 92 exit when we lost 2–1 to Sweden. There were loads of English there, with flags all over the place. After seeing Hollis we got some beers (which were cheaper than in the town) and saw England get off to a great start, going 1–0 up from a Shearer free kick. But two goals in two minutes from Sweden was the end of the scoring, and prompted a shower of beer and spit on to the Swedish fans in the lower tier. Someone even pissed in a beer glass and gave them a golden shower. England played crap after that, and at the end of the match we went out to leave the stadium, only to be kept in by loads of riot police. People threw loads of stuff at the police, who'd kept a low profile until then, and they responded with tear gas, in the corridor at the back of the stand which was only about 12 feet wide. Not surprisingly a few windows were put through, and every available sign or door was pulled off and thrown at the police. Then we realised that we could get out at the other end of the stand, so we just left along with most others.

We'd lost Hollis and Kerry, but found them when we got back to Central Station, and the five of us went for a few beers, before going back to our hotel to crash out. There were loads of riot police around the station, but I didn't see any trouble. No sign of Stockholm's famous Black Army, apparently a bunch of skinheads. We flew back the next day and found out that Darlo had won at Mansfield, and despite England losing it had been a great weekend.

In October, me and Mel went over to Luxembourg, going by coach via Dover on a package tour that only cost £89 including the hotel. The bus was cramped but we had a good laugh, and there were mostly Hull City and Sheffield United fans on our bus. One of the Blades fans kept shouting, 'For you, zie war ist over. Your hut ist second left, third Reich!' Luxembourg is a shit country though, so it's no wonder they're so much into all the EU bollocks. I counted only three good looking women in the whole of Luxembourg. Bit of a change to Sweden. We still had loads of beer, but got soaked in the ground which made Darlo's Feethams ground look like Premier League. England won 3–0, but it was a crap performance against a load of part-timers and it was summarised by chants of '3–0, we beat the bank clerks 3–0…' And then there was the chant of 'Eileen, takes it up the arse, Eileen, takes it up the arse…', referring to Eileen Drewery, Glenn Hoddle's infamous faith healer. There were loads of police in the city centre but no major trouble, and we went back to good old blighty the next day, after completing another tour of duty for our country.

England haven't exactly got off to the best of starts to the

Euro 2000 qualifiers, with four points from three games, but I'm still confident. So the next one's are Bulgaria and Poland next year. We're planning to go to Wembley for the Sweden game in June, and then fly out to Bulgaria the next day for the match four days later. Should be a nice little holiday, as Bulgaria's next to Turkey so the weather should be warm, and the beer should be cheap as well. If we go to all of the away qualifiers, then we should get tickets for all of the matches for the finals, which are in Belgium and Holland.

As I write this, Darlington have been top of the league and we've beaten the scum (Hartlepool) 2–0, but we've slipped up lately though, dropping down to mid-table. I just hope that England manage to qualify for Euro 2000, because that'll be a great laugh going over there. The change of manager might upset things though. I realise that Glen Hoddle upset many people with his remarks about disabled people, but his sacking implies that no one is allowed to have an opinion. I had my faith in Glenn Hoddle. Whilst I would have picked Paul Gascoigne for the World Cup, Hoddle seemed to know what he was doing. In Hod we trust, or so I thought! I suppose in the end he was turning into a bit of a nutcase in the public's eye. I don't think that if he'd said those remarks in early 1998 rather than 1999, after the World Cup, he would have been sacked. People were just after an excuse to get rid of him, after the 2nd round World Cup exit, his controversial diary, his faith healer, and the poor start to the Euro 2000 campaign.

People have slagged him off a lot since the World Cup, but they seem to forget the good job he did in qualifying for the World Cup, particularly the games in Italy and Poland. We were unlucky in the World Cup, and could have gone on to win it if it wasn't for a dodgy ref and some cheating

Conclusion

Argies. The press are just so keen to slag off any England manager whenever something goes wrong. We can still qualify for Euro 2000, and it would be made easier if the England manager and the players had the full support of the media. But I can understand some of the criticisms of him which suggest that he's a bit of a control freak, or a bit over confident. I suppose my choice for the new England manager would have been Terry Venables, if the FA could've persuaded him after his previous treatment. I just hope that Kevin Keegan can do the business. He's certainly a popular choice.

One thing I was shocked about was when I learnt that the two England players who missed penalties against Argentina, Paul Ince and David Batty, had never taken penalties before. Then Glenn Hoddle and John Gorman (his assistant), tell us that the England players did not practise any penalty kicks before the tournament. They even defended the policy of not practising penalties by saying that it makes no difference and can't recreate the tension and atmosphere of a penalty shoot out. What bollocks. Though they have a point, practising penalties would have greatly improved our chances of winning. Just look at the Germans and Brazilians when it comes to penalties. No one can say that they don't practise.

I thought that the reaction to David Beckham's sending off was well over the top. Fair enough, he plays for Man U, wears skirts, shags a Spice Girl and is a flash Cockney, but he's a good player and needs to be part of the England squad. People seem to forget that free kick that he scored against Colombia. And not one person in that bar in St Etienne blamed him for England going out. I blame the shit ref and cheating Argies. He was still a twat for retaliating like that though.

I didn't really have much interest in the rest of World Cup, and wanted either Holland or Denmark to win. It was great to see Germany get beat 3–0 by Croatia, and Argentina get beat by Holland, but it soon became a case of 'anyone but France'. But of course, they won it. I've not really anything much against the French, but after the fuck up with the tickets and the attitudes of the French authorities, plus the fact France are the shittest of the seven or eight teams that were tipped to win, there's no way they deserved to win it.

I'd say that there's a few songs that sum up the World Cup for me, all of which are on my tape (see Appendix 2). 'Vindaloo' represents the mad partying atmosphere of the English. 'Carnival de Paris' sums up the French feeling to it all. The BBC's theme music sums up the drama and eventual disappointment of the World Cup. And for pure depression after the Argie match, 'Walkaway' by Cast sums up the feeling.

In summary, I had a great time at the World Cup and love watching England away. Despite the actions of the French authorities and the North Africans in Marseilles, we were made to feel welcome by the French people, although they were certainly a bit paranoid about us. I watch a lot of football and always look forward to the away games, especially the ones that are further away like London. But supporting a small club like Darlington doesn't give me the chance to go abroad. Playing the Welsh teams is the nearest we get to playing in Europe. But watching England gives me the opportunity to go abroad for an away match.

Anyone who's like me, loves football, loves beer, loves travelling, loves being English, or any combination of those, will love going abroad to watch England. It's the one occasion when I can really be myself and not give a shit what people think. It's fucking brilliant! Roll on Euro 2000!

Appendix 1

The Awards

Best Pub – The London Town, Toulouse

Biggest fuck up by the French authorities – Lens, 26 June

National Anthem that sounds most like an ice-cream van – Italy

National Anthem that sounds most like a circus – Brazil

Best goal – Michael Owen, England v Argentina

Funniest goal – Morocco's third against Scotland, with Jim Leighton looking like the useless twat he is

Worst goalkeeper – Jim Leighton (see above)

Most ironic World Cup song – Scotland's 'Don't come home too soon', and they carried on the tradition of a first-round exit

Best World Cup Song – 'Vindaloo' by Fat Les

Most memorable song in the stadiums – 'The Great Escape' (England)

Best fans, in terms of taking over the towns and stadiums, and singing the best and most varied songs louder than anyone else – England, of course

Most irritating chant – '*Allez les bleus, allez les bleus*' (France)

Funniest song – 'There's only one Ronaldo, one Ronaldo, with a packet of sweets and a cheeky smile, Ronaldo is a fucking paedophile – Scotland, but also sung by us in Toulouse

Best service in a café or restaurant – the Indian in Paris.

Worst service in a café or restaurant – the café in Paris that we walked out of

Loudest fart – Day 14, the post-vindaloo/pre-shit fart in Paris

Best Frenchman – Michel, in Amsterdam

Best Character we'd met – Hollis

Most irritating and thick nationality – Americans

Person we'd least expected to meet – Yogi in Calais

Most miserable famous person we met – Arsene Wenger in Marseilles

Person who did the most shits – me

Best French city – Toulouse

Best barmaid/waitress – the one in Marseilles, near the beach, Day 2

Best match attended – England v Tunisia, Marseilles

Best stadium visited – Stade de France, St Denis

Best hotel – Trianon Wilson, Toulouse

Worst hotel – Francois the 1st, Toulouse

Appendix 1: The Awards

Worst sunburn – my head after Marseilles

Biggest wanker – the *Daily Express* reporter in Toulouse

Best train journey – Lille to Marseilles, Day 2

Most disgusting sight – seeing some wanker wearing a Hartlepool shirt in Marseilles

Best beer – the local bar in Marseilles, Day 3

Worst beer – Pizza Hut in Toulouse

Best place for women – Toulouse

Worst smell – my dirty sock bag

Best thing said to Americans – 'Shut the fuck up,' in Amsterdam

Worst hangover – Day 3, Marseilles

Spookiest person – the Russian outside the Stade de France

Worst World Cup Venue – Lens

Most told story in France – the bin incident at Cardiff

Appendix 2

Jamie's World Cup Special Tape

Side One

1 'Three Lions 98' – Skinner, Badiel and the Lightning Seeds
2 'Vindaloo' – Fat Les
3 'You'll Never Walk Alone' – The Kop
4 'Can We Kick It (no we can't)' – The Wall of Orange
5 'Three Lions (original version)' – Skinner, Badiel and the Lightning Seeds
6 'Oh Sweet England' – Bobby Moore, Geoff Hurst, Martin Peters and Nationwide England Supporters
7 'This Time (we'll get it right)' – England World Cup Squad 1982
8 'Maradona Handball' – The Business
9 'Viva Bobby Moore' – The Business
10 'World In Motion' – England/New Order
11 'You'll Never Walk Alone' – Gerry and the Pacemakers
12 'England's Glory' – England's Glory
13 'Carnival de Paris' – Dario G
14 'The Great Escape' – England Supporters Band
15 'Back Home' – England World Cup Squad 1970

Appendix 2: Jamie's World Cup Special Tape

Side Two

1 'God Save the Queen'
2 'Land of Hope and Glory'
3 'Thine Be the Glory'
4 'Rule Britannia'
5 'Jerusalem'
6 'The British Grenadiers'
7 'I Vow To Thee My Country'
8 'For He Is An Englishman'
9 'Colonel Bogey'
10 'The Great Escape'
11 '633 Squadron'
12 'Dambusters'
13 'The Guns of Navarone'
14 'The Longest Day'
15 'The Battle of Britain'
16 'Grandstand'
17 'Sports Report'
18 'Match of the Day'
19 'Pavane by Fauré' (BBC's World Cup theme)
20 'Walkaway' – Cast